People are saying…

"Ansary opens a perspective on today's political systems that helps you understand why our society is so fragmented today."

--Tania Romanov, author of *One Hundred Years of Exile: A Romanov's Search for Her Father's Russia*

"Tamim Ansary's *Truther Narratives* is an engaging, insightful analysis of what makes conspiracy theories appealing—and when they thrive best (spoiler alert: times like now). Ansary's warm, conversational tone and humor make this a book that one can enjoy despite the genuinely frightening truth, which is that conspiracy theories, or truther narratives, as he calls them, have always gained momentum in times of change, often with horrifying results for minorities and intellectuals. Still, Ansary teases out the ways that our minds can play tricks on us with sympathy for the deluded and hope for us all."

--Colleen Shoshana McKee, author of *Routine Bloodwork*

"Writer Tamim Ansary dons three hats — historian, philosopher, and raconteur — to warn us of a dangerous pattern we are experiencing today, one linked to hundreds of years of periodic societal upheavals that weaken our communal immune system, not against disease, but against vicious conspiracy theories. His page-turning book *Truther Narratives* is brilliantly crafted, taking no shortcuts despite its brevity. … The reader is taken through complex tales of widespread delusions that were accepted as fact, and outcomes that were deadly. Equally troubling are the connections he reveals, between eras, narratives, victims and perpetrators, all of it leading to our present troubles. Despite my knowledge of history, and decades as a journalist, I was unsettled by these revelations."

--Eric Nalder, Pulitzer Prize winning investigative journalist, author of *Tankers Full of Trouble, The Perilous Journey of Alaskan Crude*

Truther Narratives

Conspiracy Theory Explained

What it is
How it forms
Why it spreads

Tamim Ansary

KAJAKI
PRESS

San Francisco

Published by Kajaki Press
www.kajakipress.com

Paperback ISBN 978-0-9982623-3-8

Cover design by Todd Thomas
Additional art by Elina Ansary
First Edition

Dedicated to my parents Terttu and Amanuddin who raised me to believe that truth is a direction, not a destination. Special thanks to Jessamyn Ansary, whose editorial prowess helped give this book its shape and added coherence to my scattered thoughts.

ALSO BY TAMIM ANSARY

West of Kabul, East of New York
Destiny Disrupted
The Widow's Husband
Games Without Rules
Road Trips
The Invention of Yesterday
Sinking the Ark

"What does it feel like to be wrong? Does it feel bad? Does it feel…annoying? Awkward? Embarrassing? No. That's what it feel like in the moment that you *discover* you're wrong. But until that moment, being wrong feels exactly like being right."

Jonathan Haidt
Author of *The Righteous Mind*

Contents

Introduction 1

Truther Narratives: The Phenomenon 10

   Is "Truther" a Personality Type? 11

   The Evolution Factor 19

   The Archetypal Narrative 24

   How Narrative Works 42

      Our Stories, Our Selves 45

   How Narratives Go Wrong 50

   The Virus Metaphor...56

The Truther Narrative in History...64

   Two Protypes Are Born 65

      The Jewish Moneylender...66

      The Knights Templars 73

   What the Similarities Suggest..82

      Social Paradigm 89

   After the Paradigm Shift 92

      Rosicrucians...96

      Masons 99

      Illuminati 102

   The French Revolution and Its Aftermath 105

   World History—the Truthers' Version 109

      Two Prototypes Merge 114

How History (Actually) Happens 120

   Tipping Points 121

   Ripple Effects 124

   Chaos Theory 124

   Black Swans 127

Clues from History 129

   The Abstraction of Money 131

   When the Social Paradigm Is Shifting 133

Our World, Our Time 136

Why Now? 137

   Countries 137

   Cyberspace 138

   Nature 140

   Children 141

   Machines 143

   The Digitized Life 145

   Gender 146

   Culture 146

   Togetherness 148

   The Story We Are In 149

   The Noise 154

   The Music 155

Introduction

One day in 2016, a young man browsing the Internet saw something that filled him with righteous rage. He read that in Washington D.C. there was a pizzeria called Comet Ping Pong which served pizza upstairs but in the basement, unbeknownst to the public, it hosted a pedophilia ring catering exclusively to the wealthy power elite of the city, the very people running the country.

"The world is too afraid to act," Edgar Welch told his friends, "and I'm too stubborn not to." He loaded up on guns, drove to the nation's capital, and burst into Comet Ping Pong, determined to put an end to this horror. He fired three shots into the walls and tried to find the door to the basement but there was no basement. Comet Ping Pong just sold pizza. When the police arrived, Welch admitted that "The intel on this wasn't a hundred percent."

Looking back at "Pizzagate", as it came to be known, many of us no doubt chuckle and shake our heads. The whole thing was just a conspiracy theory, one of those crazy stories that pop up on the Internet.

Many of us, perhaps, but not all. There are people even now, it seems, who, upon reading words like these, are apt to think: how do we know it was just a conspiracy theory? Maybe the entrance to the basement was an underground tunnel from another building. Maybe the pedophiles had advance word that the cops were coming and cleared out just in time to—

Let's pause for a moment and focus on that question: how do we know?

The dictionary tells us that a conspiracy is a plot by two or more people to do something unsavory or illegal. Garden-variety conspiracies answering to this description take place all the time. I'd bet serious money there are numerous ones big and small underway right now. But when we call a speculation a "Conspiracy Theory", it's not these garden variety conspiracies we're referring to. When we hang that label on a story, we're declaring it debunked.

Whenever we suspect that a real conspiracy is underway, it's quite proper to call for an investigation and search out evidence that will show whether the allegation is true or not. But when we say of some allegation, "oh, that's just a conspiracy theory," we're saying the search for evidence can stop. We're saying we've already recognized this as one of those cockamamie stories that are false by definition.

But if a Conspiracy Theory is false by definition, shouldn't we be able to state that definition? What exactly are the traits of a false-by-definition Conspiracy Theory vs. a merits-looking-into suspicion that some people are colluding with some other people to carry out some nefarious scheme?

When I asked people I knew for a definition, none of them came up with a satisfactory answer. Based on my survey, it would seem that no one believes a Conspiracy Theory. If they know it's a Conspiracy Theory they don't believe it. If they believe it, they don't classify it as a Conspiracy Theory. Everybody I talked to knew of *other* people who believed in Conspiracy Theories. One of my friends said there was no need to define Conspiracy Theory because we all kinda' recognize one when we see one. But that's the trouble. We're not all part of the same "we-all". In America as a whole, we certainly don't all agree on what to classify as a false-by-definition Conspiracy Theory. Consider the following list:

- The Moon Landing was fake.
- 9/11 was an inside job.
- The JFK Assassination was a government plot.
- The government is infecting people with a deadly disease in order to study them.
- Vaccines cause autism.
- Malaysia Airlines Flight 370 was hijacked by a terrorist group operating from secret headquarters in Central Asia.
- FDR knew about Pearl Harbor and let it happen.
- Ten foot lizards from an alien planet rule the world.
- The 2020 election was stolen.
- Donald Trump is a Russian asset.
- Certain big pharmaceutical companies conspired to get Americans addicted to painkillers they knew to be deadly.
- Black helicopters seen in Idaho are actually a new life form created in a lab by the United Nations to spy on Americans.
- Birds aren't real.
- The Earth is flat, not round.

3

Which of these are the obviously false "just-a-conspiracy-theory" type of stories and which are possible real conspiracies that might be worth looking into further? In order to discuss this issue, what we need first of all is a term, a term that doesn't refer to just any speculation alleging a reprehensible collusion but one that refers specifically to this false-by-definition type of conspiracy theory we're talking about here.

So I'll coin one. In this book, I'll use the term Truther Narrative for this type of thing, whatever it is. You've probably heard of "9/11 Truthers", who claim that 9/11 was an inside job carried out by America's secret government. That story's one example of a Truther Narrative. Another might be that the Earth is actually flat. People who push that one would be Flat-Earth Truthers. And there are vaccine-truthers and JFK-truthers and so on and so on and so on.

My friend said we recognize a Truther Narrative when we see one, even if we can't define it. I don't deny this. I only ask: what traits are tipping us off?

Probably most of us would agree that the ten-foot lizards from an alien planet thing is a Truther Narrative—one of those false-by-definition conspiracy theories. It's just so preposterous. But is that the trait that all Truther Narratives have in common? Preposterosity? (To coin a term.) In that case, what about the theory that the moon landing was faked? No supernatural threads, no sci-fi elements. Movie studios routinely create realistic portrayals of things that aren't actually happening. If they can make a film showing gladiators duking it out in ancient Rome, why not a false but realistic portrayal of men landing on the moon?

I suppose most of us would call the faked-moon-landing story false because of the absurd complexity that would be needed to pull it off: too many people would have to have been in on the plot. It's implausible that all of them, even peripheral figures, even best-boys and gaffers, even set-carpenters, janitors and gofers would have kept their involvement in such a bizarre scam a secret and taken it to their very graves.

So is that the trait one sees in all Truther Narratives? They're implausible?

In that case what would you say if someone told you that a group of the most respected senators in the country were secretly plotting to murder the chief executive in broad daylight on the Senate floor where everyone could see them do it? Just a Truther Narrative? Tell it to Julius Caesar.

Implausible might screen out the fake-moon-landing, or a modern-day follow-up to Caesar's assassination, but does it debunk the story touted by U.S. congressman Louie Gohmert in 2017, alleging that Hillary Clinton and a far-flung web of co-conspirators plotted to sell America's precious radioactive materials to Putin's Russia?

If so, how can we distinguish that narrative from the one Robert Mueller was investigating at that same time, which alleged that Donald Trump had colluded with people in Putin's Russia to influence the U.S. presidential election in his favor? What makes one of them a Truther Narrative and the other a speculation that a conspiracy worth looking into might be underway? If we can just tell, *how* can we "just tell"? What traits are we noticing?

Does the answer lie in convoluted complexity? After all, when one floats a conspiracy theory that has no truth to it, holes soon show up, because reality is complex. You have to patch the holes, but then holes show up in the patches, and you have to add more patches, whereupon holes turn up in those, and so on and so on.

In order to believe Gohmert's Hillary Clinton theory, for example, you'd have to envision a diagram such as this—which Gohmert actually did present to the House Judiciary Committee, hoping to illustrate the connections comprising the alleged web of conspirators.

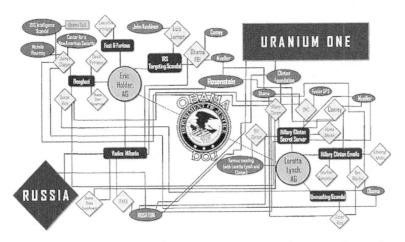

But the convoluted complexity of a theory cannot ipso facto unmask it as false. Consider the Iran/Contra affair of the eighties, a conspiracy we know to be true because it was thoroughly unmasked. The co-conspirators included:

- the Reagan Administration;
- the anti-government guerillas in Nicaragua;
- a cabal of private U.S. arms manufacturing businessmen;
- a secret group within the U.S intelligence establishment;
- the Israeli military intelligence services;
- the Islamist revolutionaries who had just seized control in Iran; and
- Lebanon's radical Islamist party Hezbollah.

Implausible? Check. Convoluted? Check. Complex? Check. It's not just that all these disparate parties were involved in the same *drama*. They were all on the same side of the plot—Israel's Mossad was colluding with Hezbollah was colluding with the Contras of Nicaragua was colluding with people in the government of Egypt was colluding with Khomeini was colluding with private arms manufacturers in Virginia was colluding with officials in the Reagan Administration—everything about this theory screams implausible. But this one really happened. We know, because the plot unraveled.

So if convoluted complexity doesn't mark a story as a Truther Narrative, what does? Is it a lurid tone that gives a narrative away? Take, for instance, the theory that AIDS was created in a lab by the CIA to wipe out African Americans and gay men. Who but a comic book villain like Modok[1] would do a thing like that?

Ah, but this is where we must be cautious. People *have* done things like that, not in comic books but in real life. In 1932, for

---

[1] Modok inhabits the universe of Marvel Comics. The name is an acronym standing for Mechanical Organism Designed Only for Killing.

example, the Public Health Service teamed up with scientists at the Tuskegee Institute in Alabama to run a study of 600 Black men. Some 400 of these men had syphilis, the rest were the control group. All of them were told they would be receiving medicine for a condition they supposedly had, called bad blood. Actually they were receiving a placebo, nothing more. The study wasn't about medicine, it was about syphilis. The researchers were interested in observing how the disease progressed if left untreated. After a cure for syphilis was found, these subjects were not told about it. They continued receiving the placebo until they died. The experiment went on for some forty years. It didn't come out until the 1970s, when investigative journalists dug up the truth and published stories.

I don't know about you, but to me, the Tuskegee study sounds as luridly villainous as could be. The scientists involved were keeping their study secret from the public because they must have known it was villainous. This all fits the dictionary definition of conspiracy. And if journalists of the time had suspected what the scientists were up to and written articles setting forth their suspicions, they would have been presenting a theory and the theory would have alleged that a conspiracy was underway. So technically speaking, if readers had responded to these articles by saying, "Oh, that's just a conspiracy theory" they would have been correct, semantically speaking.

But the way we use the term nowadays, "That's a conspiracy theory" means: the search for evidence can stop. It means: investigating these allegations would be a waste of time because we already know this one to be false.

In the case of something like the Tuskegee study, however, it's vital that the search for evidence *not* stop. In a case like that, an investigation *should* proceed. That's why it's vital that we define exactly what we're talking about, when we talk about Truther Narratives.

Part One

Truther Narratives:
The Phenomenon

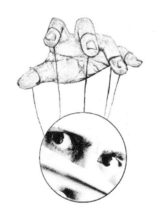

Is "Truther" a Personality Type?

Many people who scoff at Truther Narratives do so on intellectual grounds. They treat the belief in a given Truther Narrative as a mistake because they're thinking of it in the way we think of news reports, historical accounts, political analyses, scientific explanations, and other nonfiction. If you're approaching a Truther Narrative in this way, it's relevant to ask "What's the evidence?" because that's how you correct a mistake. You find the flawed evidence, you spot the broken logic, and you show the person where they went wrong.

But if you look at "Truther Narrative" as a certain type of story, a different question emerges. Instead of asking, 'Why can't they see how implausible that story is,' you'd be asking, 'Why are they drawn to that story?' Because that's the elephant in the room. If it's true that "we all recognize a Truther Narrative when we see one," the further truth is that some people are drawn to what they see and some people are not. In fact, some are even repelled. Why is that? Could it reflect two different personality types? Are some people helplessly drawn to a Truther Narrative because that's just the kind of people they are, the way some people find romance novels to their taste and others prefer legal thrillers?

Political scientist Richard Hofstadter pointed in this direction, I suppose, with his classic essay published in 1964,

The Paranoid Style in American Politics. Writers following in his footsteps made "paranoid" the qualifier of choice for this false-by-definition type of conspiracy theory we're examining here. "Paranoid" implies that the difference between a Truther Narrative and a hypothesis that some unsavory conspiracy might be underway isn't in the theory being spun, it's in the person spinning the theory.

Was Hofstadter onto something? Well, there *is* evidence to suggest that yes, he might have been. For one thing, people who believe in one Truther Narrative tend to believe in many others as well. When Canadian reporter Jonathan Kay interviewed people who believed that 9/11 was an inside job (for his book *Among the Truthers*) he found that most of them also believed that a secret group within the government assassinated JFK.

When a team of Austrian psychologists investigated belief in Truther Narratives, they found that people who believed the moon landing was faked also tended to believe that the energy drink Red Bull was made from an illegal and highly addictive substance derived from bull testicles that made lab rats grow wings. The researchers knew this story to be false because they themselves had just made it up—for their survey. What's more, as best I can tell, using that story in their survey was like releasing an invasive species into the wild: once it was out there, it spread and spread (and today you can still find it touted in obscure corners of the Internet.)

I know, I know: that's all anecdotal. But according to psychologist Rob Brotherton, research has consistently found that people who believe in one conspiracy theory tend to believe in many others as well. Brotherton has a doctorate in psychology, he specializes in conspiracy theory, and he lectures on the subject at Barnard and Columbia Universities, so I'll take his word for it.[2] Research cited by Brotherton seems to suggest that it's not this or that particular conspiracy theory people are drawn to but Truther Narrative as a *type* of story. To paraphrase my friend, these people recognize a Truther Narrative when they see one— and they're drawn to it as moths to candles. But why?

Brotherton offers some further clues. In many such studies, he says, researchers don't just give people a list of conspiracy theories and ask which ones they believe. They give their subjects a list of conspiracy theories ranging from totally bonkers to utterly plausible and ask them to rate *how* believable they find each one, on a scale from one to seven. The presumption is, most people's ratings will vary widely depending on what the various theories allege. If a person thinks climate change is a hoax, there's no evidence-based reason why they should also think the Queen of England plotted the assassination of Prince Di. These are two completely different stories. The overlap between the types of evidence needed to confirm or disprove each one is zero: there is no overlap. None.

---

[2] For further information about the studies cited here, see *Suspicious Minds, Why We Believe in Conspiracy Theories.* by Rob Brotherton. Bloomsbury, London, 2015.

Yet according to Brotherton, when studies of this type have been done, they've found that in many cases—too many to be mere coincidence—people who give one conspiracy theory a rating of 7 tend to give all the others on the list a similarly high score. People who totally dismiss one conspiracy theory tend to give all the others a low score as well. The pattern extends even to the middle numbers. If one theory gets a three, they all get a three or thereabouts. I say "tends to" because we're talking about statistical correlations here, but the correlation is strong enough to suggest that people come to Truther Narrative with a predisposition. Their judgment of believability has less to do with the details of any particular story and more to do with the attitudes and ideas they bring to their judgment.

Consider the curious case of Bin Laden, dead and alive. In 2012, psychologists Mike Wood and Karen Douglas found that there were three different accounts floating around on the Internet about how and when Osama Bin Laden died. They read that:

1. Bin Laden was killed by U.S. Navy Seals in Abbottabad, Pakistan, on May 11, 2011.
2. Bin Laden died of Marfan disease in Afghanistan in 2002.
3. Bin Laden's death was faked: he's still alive and in hiding.

So Wood and Douglas did a survey asking people to rate how believable they found each of these three accounts, on a scale from not-at-all to yes-indeed-totally. In their paper *Dead and Alive*, they reported that people who believed Theory 1 tended to regard the other two as bunkum. But: people who *doubted* Theory 1, tended to believe the other two about equally.

Huh? How's that again? They were equally ready to believe that Bin Laden was alive and that he died many years ago? How could that be?

Easy macheesi. The answer could be that they weren't choosing among three beliefs but two:

> The official story is true.
> The official story is false.

When those are the only two categories, what look like two contradictory beliefs are essentially the same belief. "Bin Laden is alive" and "Bin Laden died long ago" both mean "Something Fishy Is Going On Here". Some people, it seems, are simply more prone to this kind of suspicion. It might be a personality type. Any special attraction they have to Truther Narratives might not reflect their evaluation of the story as true. It might reflect their sense of what the world is like and how the story fits in with that picture. If that's the case, the suspicion they feel probably wasn't created by the story. It was there before they read the story. The suspicion they feel is probably like an itch they have and have had all along, an itch in want of scratching. Apparently, Truther Narrative delivers the kind of scratching they crave, the kind that relieves that particular itch, at least temporarily.

Everyone is suspicious sometimes, and there are times when suspicion is warranted, but a propensity for constant suspicion doesn't seems like it represents a given person's response to a particular thing happening out there; it seems more like it signals something happening inside the person.

If attraction to Truther Narratives correlates to a certain personality type, you'd expect that people drawn to such narratives would have other traits in common too. And Brotherton tells us that when social scientists have looked into this question, they *have* found discernible patterns. One trait such believers seem to share is a propensity for spotting hidden patterns, hidden order. If researchers show them a drawing like the one below and ask them to find a hidden picture, they're likely to spot the sailboat. Do you see it? So do I. Most of us would.

But the type of person drawn to Truther Narratives might also spot a sailboat in this next picture. Do you see it?

Me neither. I guess we're just not the type.

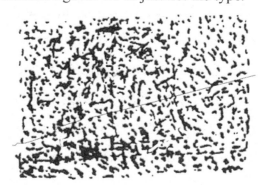

What else do believers in Truther Narrative have in common? Well, research suggests the following tendencies.

- They see the world in more black-and-white terms than most people, less in shades of gray.
- They see intention where there isn't any. Think: Robert De Niro in *Taxi Driver:* "Are you looking at *me*? Are *you* looking at *me?*"
- They see random events as connected. If a dog barks over there and a man on a bicycle runs into a tree over here, they're apt to think the dog's barking caused the bicycle accident.
- They tend to sense danger where none exists. This is the big one, of course; this is the paranoia Hofstadter was speaking about.

The question arises, then: could an attraction to Truther Narrative indicate some underlying personality disorder?

Instead of wasting time and energy debunking Truther Narratives, should we be formulating a 12-step program to rescue Truthers (aka people who all-too-readily believe in conspiracy theories) from their propensity to embrace such stories?

The Evolution Factor

Ah, but here's the conundrum. Taken individually, these traits are ones we all possess to some extent or another. Evolution built them into our biological makeup for damn good reasons. Far from being liabilities, these traits have kept us alive through the ages. If we didn't have them, at least to some extent, we'd probably be extinct by now.

Take, for example, seeing danger where none exists.

We emerged into humanhood as bands of primates roaming the wilderness, looking for food, while keeping one eye out for predators. The most dangerous of dangers were those so stealthy, they could sneak up without a sound. A person alert to predators that stealthy would be among the first to notice them when they did first become detectible.

If you saw danger where there was no evidence of any, you would sometimes be wrong. And sure, this might have negative social consequences for you at times. Some people might call you a coward, some might laugh at you, some might lecture you about the boy who cried wolf. But that doesn't mean you and your group would be better off without this propensity. Being wrong only means your radar wasn't perfect. It would be like getting some of the letters wrong in an eye chart. Okay, so your vision is less than 20/20, that doesn't mean eyes are a defect and you should pluck yours out.

As for spotting patterns where no pattern exists?

Well, a person who does this is merely going one step beyond spotting patterns that are very hard to see. This is merely an overactive version of another vital evolutionary survival trait: spotting patterns in a riot of random data. And sure, a person whose needle is over-sensitive might sometimes mistake a log for a crocodile. Ha ha, look at that moron, running for his life from a log. A person who is *not* good at this might mistake a crocodile for a log. Wow, look at Joe Cool over there, sitting right on a crocodile's jaw!

Which of these two is more likely to get eaten by a crocodile, the moron or Joe Cool? Which will likely add more of their DNA to the gene pool? No wonder evolution kept this propensity on the edge of too much rather than on the borders of too-little.

The same goes for the other propensities mentioned above. Seeing intention where none exists? That's just an overamped version of spotting intentions at all. We humans *must* detect other people's intentions, because the landscape we inhabit isn't geographical so much as social.

Steering through a social landscape requires that we know what other people might be thinking or wanting. Often we have to guess, because intention is not a substance the senses can directly detect, and other people aren't always eager to advertise their intentions. You might have to make your guesses based on inadvertent clues. If your needle is too sensitive, you might over-guess at times and spot intentions that aren't there. That's not good, but it's better than *failing* to spot, say, a *hostile* intention where one *does* exist.

Then there's this business of seeing random events as connected. This one is crucial, actually. Without this propensity, we couldn't construct stories. A story is a series of causally-connected events that form a single whole. Sure there are other, more sophisticated ways to describe a story, but this one's basic. If events aren't at least causally connected, they don't form a story. And if they are causally connected, then, in addition to being a bunch of discrete events, they are parts of some single whole.

Among its many functions, storytelling is how we humans build a worldview, and building a shared worldview is how we humans bring into existence the group-selves that we mostly are. In fact, as individuals, we humans are mere cells of various and numerous group-selves that exist as social entities.

It's mostly as group selves that we take action in the world. If we couldn't form these group-selves, we would never have emerged as the fearsome species we have proven to be. Over the course of history, in the competition among human groups, the ones who had more of this trait tended to win, live long, and leave behind more progeny. Evolution has selected for this trait because it makes disparate individuals better able to function as if they were a single creature and thereby to carry out shared intentions. Narrative is the key here.

A Truther Narrative delivers a narrative. The problem is, so does a news story. So does a biography. So does a novel. So does a history. So does a scripted movie. So does a documentary movie. So does a joke. There are many different kinds of narratives, and they have many particular criteria by which we judge them.

The most sweeping and perhaps most obvious divide, however, is between fiction and nonfiction. We take this distinction to be fundamental and obvious, but it's actually more ambiguous than we commonly suppose. When we read a nonfiction narrative we demand that the facts presented be accurate and true. When we watch or read or hear a fictional narrative, we still want truth, but the truth we're looking for is thematic, not factual. We don't throw the Odyssey away because it turns out no such person ever actually existed. We look to fiction for experiences that evoke and illuminate our own emotional truths.

Narrative, however, in and of itself, has mechanisms and drives and triggers and patterns that make it work, whether it be fiction or nonfiction. This, I submit is what makes Truther Narrative so inherently problematic. A Truther Narrative presents itself to the world as nonfiction, and it must. The central promise of every conspiracy theory is that it is *not* fiction. Its most strident claim is that *this* is what's *really* going on. But the core function of the Truther Narrative is to invoke an emotional experience, something that is properly the domain of fiction.

When fiction is effective, when it's working effectively, it is built around thematic structures that aren't visible on the surface. The underlying scaffolding hidden within false-by-definition conspiracy theories of every type is the archetypal structure that I am calling "the Truther Narrative".

The Archetypal Narrative

I first got interested in conspiracy theory in the early 1980s. I don't mean this or that particular conspiracy theory, I mean the phenomenon as a whole. I became aware of it one day in Turkey, when I stumbled across a pamphlet purporting to reveal the "secret meaning" of history. The pamphlet said this secret had to do with Jews... and with Masons...and with Rosicrucians...and it went on to name several other parties implicated in a dark, gigantic plot with roots going back to the days of the Egyptian pharaohs. The people who published this pamphlet called themselves Muslims, but what they were touting wasn't Islam, to my mind. It was ... I didn't know what to call it: something else.

Whatever it was, I saw it again one night on cable TV, in America, in the person of a televangelist, ranting about the end times. This time it was wearing Christianity as its camouflage, but it wasn't Christianity either. It was...something else.

Whatever it was, this something-else, I glimpsed it again one day, in the rantings of a cluster of self-proclaimed atheist "revolutionaries" on a street corner, shouting through a bullhorn their notion of who *really* controlled the world. This time, it was masquerading as a quasi-Marxist political analysis but it wasn't really an analysis of any kind. It was... something else.

What struck me about these narratives wasn't that they sounded true. They didn't to me; not at all. Not one single bit. What struck me was a certain flavor they had, a flavor that reminded me of the cult phenomenon of the mid-1970s.

In that decade, quite a number of people I knew got sucked into groups such as Scientology, Lifespring, the Rajneesh cult, and others. Some of these people I knew vaguely, some I knew quite well. In 1974, give or take, a number of people I knew personally flung away their possessions and went to meet up with a cultish couple known as "The Two", who were telling people they were messengers from the Mother Ship, coming to save humanity.

A few years later, I met people who knew people who joined a cult founded by Jim Jones and followed him to Guyana, where all 900-plus of them committed suicide over the course of two horrific days in 1978.

A few decades later, I saw in the news that The Two, the couple I had glancingly encountered in the mid-70s, had devolved into a tiny cult called Heavens Gate, and they too had committed collective suicide, although by then the group had dwindled to just a couple of dozen believers, none of whom were people I'd known. I'm guessing their Mother Ship never came.

People who joined these cults didn't think they were joining a cult. To them, "cult" was the outsiders' term. They themselves described their experience as a sudden discovery of a blinding truth. These cults were diverse. They had different programs, different messages, different structures, and yet in some way, I confess, they felt somehow identical to me. It was something about the appeal they exerted, the mechanisms built into them to suck people in, and the mechanisms whereby they held onto them once they'd gotten them. There were many cults but there was also, it seemed to me, some single underlying cult phenomenon. Certain social conditions, it seemed, generated this phenomenon the way certain biological conditions generate spots of mold.

The Truther Narrative phenomenon I began to notice in the 80s gave me traces of this same feeling. After I read the pamphlet mentioned above, I encountered other Truther Narratives. They'd probably been lurking around all along, but once I began to notice them, I kept noticing more of them, and the more of them I noticed, the more they began to seem like particular instances of some single phenomenon. This is the phenomenon I want to get at in this book, at the heart of which is this complex of ideas that we treat as false-by-definition but for which, until now, we have had no label except the same two words the dictionary assigns to any garden variety conspiracy theory, at least some of which are not at all "false-by-definition".

The thing is, when we call a speculation a Conspiracy Theory, we're not just saying we beg to differ. There's an odor of derogatory judgement clinging to the two words joined to form this term. We're not just saying the theory in question is wrong; we're saying there's something wrong with believing in this theory. Some writers who use the term conspiracy theory skirt the issue by distinguishing between two kinds of conspiracy theory, the kind that's okay and the kind that's not-okay. They most often do this by adding some qualifier, some term such as "unsubstantiated" or the oft-heard "baseless" to the kind that's not-okay. But these terms are too weak to be of service. If some dead-bang documentary evidence were to turn up tomorrow proving that three men working for the CIA secretly colluded to help Oswald assassinate JFK, would that suddenly turn all those conspiracy theorists of the past 70 years into not-conspiracy theorists retroactively? You see the problem.

Others add some version of "crazy" as a qualifier. That, however, assumes that what I'm calling the Truther Narrative is found only among disconnected losers on the fringes of society. It's found there, to be sure, but is it only there? When disagreement about what is and what isn't a Truther Narrative divides tens of millions of people into non-overlapping camps, the crazy label is a socially problematic way of marking out which conspiracy theories are Truther Narratives and which are legitimate speculations about possible conspiracies.

I say, the key to unravelling this riddle is to start by looking at Truther Narratives purely as story. Forget for a moment whether any particular one holds water as a description of reality, the standard we quite properly apply to a news story or a political analysis or a cookbook. Let's approach Truther Narratives as a literary critic would: instead of focusing on content and evidence, let's ask: what do all false-by-definition narratives of this type share in terms of structure and purpose? What mechanisms give them shape and make them function as whatever-the-hell-they-are?

I'm proposing that when we use the term conspiracy theory as a conversation stopper—"oh, shut up, that's just a conspiracy theory"—we're identifying the singled-out story as a categorical *kind* of story. We're recognizing, within this particular conspiracy theory, an archetypal template I'm calling: Truther Narrative.

For a crude analogy. think of genre fiction, especially the kind that people often dismiss as "formulaic". Just a page or two into such a work and you probably recognize what kind of story you're heading into: is it a romance novel, a legal thriller, a police procedural, a sword-and-sorcery epic…? You might not be able to identify what clues have tipped you off, but you sense what sort of story it will be, and so in an abstract sense what elements you'll encounter, where the story will go, and how it will get there. A story map stripped of all particulars is embedded in your instincts, and it lets you recognize what kind of fictional terrain you're entering.

If you enjoy romantic comedies, the archetypal story map embedded in your sensibilities gives you expectations as you follow the story. They trigger enjoyments particular to the genre as the story unfolds for you. If you're a rom-com fan, you don't know *exactly* where the story will go when you start, but you know the experience you want to have as you're reading and what feeling you want to have when it's over. Producing this feeling is the genre storyteller's job. If it's legal thrillers you're a fan of, it will be a different archetypal template activating your responses, different emotions the story will arouse. The expert storyteller has an intuitive grasp of your expectations and how to manipulate them. This is how story structure operates. This is how expert genre storytellers get rich: by using story to provoke emotions that their audiences want to feel.

But genre is only a crude metaphor. We can look to more specific story templates for a more precise analogy. Consider what we mean when we say "a Cinderella story." We don't mean the story's protagonist is named Cinderella. Her name might be Margaret, or Zuleikha or Pudding-face. She might not even be a girl but a boy. The wicked stepmother might be an investment banker, the fairy godmother a charitable foundation. But we know the protagonist has been treated as a worthless nobody. We know this character has virtues that have gone tragically unrecognized. We know a miraculous intervention is going to take this character right to the top! The Mets winning the World Series in 1969—now there was a Cinderella Story!

What we mean when we say "Cinderella Story" is not about particulars. It's something structural: a shape the story has, a setup that loads it emotionally, a payoff it delivers, and a way in which it delivers that payoff. It's completely different from a Horatio Alger story—even though both feature a rags-to-riches trajectory. The Horatio Alger story is explicitly *not* about a miracle but about doing-it-yourself:

hard work, pluck, and honesty is what takes the poor boy from the streets to the boardroom: no fairy godmother need apply: you can do it, yes *you.*

Or consider the rage-release story: a good guy is making his way through a harsh world. Don't mess with this guy, he has certain skills. And there's a bad guy; or a bunch of bad guys. They do things that no nice person would. They remind you of people who've made you angry in real life, only they're worse. And they just keep proving how bad they are in the story by piling on the bad deeds … and your outrage builds…and then the good guy enters the scene. Get ready for some rage-release.

You can discern this underlying archetypal story in some movie playing in a theater near you right now. I'm not going to name the movie because it'll be gone next month, but there'll be another one in its place, a movie with a different name and different actors and a different plot on the surface, but underlyingly it will be the same movie: because I'm not actually talking about a particular movie but a type of movie, a story built around an archetypal template.

The Odyssey, a story first told some 2,700 years ago, was built on this template. You know the one. Poor Odysseus, trying to find his way home from The War, buffeted by storms and monsters, while a bunch of assholes called "the suitors" are crowding into his home back in Ithaca, gobbling up his food, disrespecting his son, and uproariously competing to force his wife into a marriage that will give them ownership of everything Odysseus ever possessed and loved—including his wife's body.

And then Odysseus arrives.

But the story hasn't fully ripened yet. You the listener don't have enough rage built up to enjoy the full repast. So Odysseus arrives disguised as a pitiful beggar, and the suitors, true to form, make fun of this seemingly defenseless creature, kick him around, lose any claim they might have had to mercy—and that's when Odysseus picks up his bow. Holy shit—run, suitors!—too late. Odysseus has locked the doors. And the arrows start to fly.

You don't need any of Homer's particulars to experience the satisfactions this story delivers and you don't have to go back 2,700 years. You can experience the same story-satisfactions in any of the *Taken* movies starring Liam Neeson: *he*, we learn, "has certain skills." You can feel this same thrum coming from the underlying template in pretty much any Jack Reacher novel by Lee Childs.

In this same way, inside every so-called conspiracy theory is that archetypal template I'm calling the Truther Narrative. Stripped of all particulars, the Truther Narrative in full tells the following tale:

- What *seems* to be happening isn't what's *really* happening.
- What's really happening is, a Cabal is in control.
- Few know the Cabal exists because they operate through false fronts and puppets.

- You're one of the smart ones, though. *You* know that:
- There is a "They".
- "They" control the world through money.
- "They" control most sources of information.
- "They" stage news events that look real but are actually scripted and staged.
- "They" can place agents among us—so any of us might actually be one of *them*.
- "They" are evil and are acting on behalf of ultimate evil.
- The individual Cabal members are human, however—so "They" can be killed.
- But the Cabal is about to finalize its grip—so hurry! Time is running out!

I submit that such a template can float about among the countless stories of a culture unseen, like a jellyfish floating about in seawater. The archetype, as I said, is not itself directly visible. Underlying archetypes never are. They're only visible when they incarnate as particular stories. Any particular Truther Narrative might deviate from the full template in this way or that way. Any particular embodiment of the archetype might have this or that additional doodad or might be missing this or that plank—but the underlying template is down there in the collective cultural unconscious, like one of those archetypes Carl Jung talked about. At the very least, it might be compared to the thing we call "a formula" when we talk about genre fiction. It exerts pressure on the visible story to become "a better story"—i.e. conform more exactly to the archetype.

In the rage-release story you can see quite clearly how the story invokes emotions that the audience feels traces of already, brings them to the surface to build a craving for certain fantasized satisfactions, and then delivers those satisfactions. If it's done well, it's literature, if it's done so crudely that the machinery shows, it's formulaic fiction. The underlying template (stripped of all particulars) is the same in either case.

And the thing is, a powerful template of this kind guides a storyteller's telling of a story. It influences the shape the story takes as it's being told and re-told. An archetypal myth floating about in culture has what might be called a gravitational force. It can tug on strands of story floating about and weave them into the fabric of another story. The Truther Narrative can pull into its vortex whole stories that have elements of the archetype and reconfigure them into classic Truther Narratives, even though they may not have originated as "stories" at all but as real events reported in the news.

Yes, they may have started out as news events, but when someone hears a piece of news and tells it someone else, who then tells it to someone else, who then tells it to someone else, that piece of news is in the process of becoming a story. People retelling the news need not be trying to change it, they might not even be conscious of changing anything, they might just be trying to tell it well, tell it better, tell it in a way that brings out the dramatic qualities that make it so worth passing on; but the qualities that make a given story a "better story" are vested in the underlying archetypal template: and those are mechanisms that make a story work as *story*, not as news. And so, as reports of a news event pass from one teller to another to another, the archetype becomes the scaffolding that shapes the form it takes eventually—as story.

This is why Truther Narrative has a quality reminiscent of folk tales and mythology. A myth is a structure that emerges in stories that start out as stories and circulate as such within a closed network of people. The mythic structure emerges as each new teller of the tale tells it in their own way as well as they think the story can be told. If they tell it *really* well, their listeners remember it and retell it—in *their* own ways. Each new teller feels free to emphasize details that made it powerful to *them*, subtract elements that felt dull or irrelevant to *them*, shape the tale as their intuitions direct, all in service to making it "a better story". Since a whole social network is creating the story, the story is shaped by the archetypal myth embedded in the sensibility the whole network shares. The "best story" is the one that best evokes an emotion these people have in common and want to experience communally.

What sets Truther Narrative apart from myth, from genre fiction, and from story templates in general is that people don't think of it as a story they're telling. They think of it as a truth the news should be reporting but isn't. They think of themselves as researchers or investigators or journalists, not as storytellers.

This is, at least in part, what makes Truther Narratives so troublesome in the modern context—for in recent decades, at least in America and perhaps in much of the world, the distinction between fiction and nonfiction has been blurring. Think: fans howling and cheering at live WWF events, even though they all know it's fake. Think: entertainment values invading news reporting. Think: reality TV. In a world where the border between fiction and nonfiction is indistinct or dissolving, Truther Narrative is sure to have a heyday.

They plant agents among us.

Some of us are actually "them"

Versions of the archetypal Truther Narrative have been popping up in Western civilization for at least 800 years; in fact, it might have been haunting societies for as long as there have been societies held together by shared stories. Today, in any case, the web is certainly infested with people spouting Truther Narratives that are partial or sometimes full-fledged incarnations of the fundamental Truther Narrative set forth above. It started pretty much as soon as the web was born, but in recent times (it seems to me) online conspiracy theories have been converging toward ever more unadulterated expressions of that mythic archetype. A public blog I ran across recently, for example, informed me that "the battle to free humanity from a cult of human-sacrificing Satan worshipers (Ba'al, Molech, etc.) is reaching a key turning point as intense battles rage on multiple fronts."

The blogger went on to describe the battle as "a struggle between the masses allied with the military of most countries against a deeply entrenched top-level elite." He said no mass arrests have taken place yet because of "a millennia-old control system" and then offered a byzantine tangle of a diagram showing what the entrenched top-level elite controls: banks, news outlets, government agencies, movie studios, and more, much more.

The Ba'al and Moloch this blogger referenced are Babylonian gods castigated in the Bible. It's no surprise they were cited, for a Truther Narrative, properly understood, is not really a theory at all. That is to say, it's not really an attempt to explain anything—not politically, not historically, not scientifically, nor in any other way. The archetypal Truther Narrative template set forth above is more akin to a belief system, a faith, a religion.

A religious narrative isn't competing with science or scholarly historical research to prove or disprove any material fact. It isn't ultimately out to fix any material problem. What it promises to remedy is an illness of the soul: the discomfort of living in a world without meaning. Challenging a Truther Narrative by arguing against its "evidence" is like demanding from a devout religious believer hard evidence that his or her God exists in the same way as that rock over there.

Please note, however: I am not saying that Truther Narrative *is* a religion, only that it is *akin* to a religion in a certain way. And here's the similarity: to the religious believer, it doesn't matter if God is or isn't like that rock over there. To the believer, *that* question is trivial. What matters is how believing in that God makes the world feel to the believer. Science gathers evidence in order to reach a conclusion. Religion begins with a conclusion and uses it to determine what evidence should be gathered.

This makes a Truther Narrative non-falsifiable. For the person who's embraced (or been infected by) a Truther Narrative, the core proposition is axiomatically true. It is the point of departure. One does gather evidence, and the believer agrees that evidence *should* be gathered, but not in order to see if the axiom is true, because that's the given of all givens, the irreducible first fact. One uses that first fact to measure the truth or falsity of any *other* statement. If a statement fits in with the first-fact, it might be true—we just have to see *how* it fits. But if it contradicts the first fact, we can dismiss it without further ado for we know it can't be true.

For example, for the millions who believed the U.S. presidential election of 2020 was rigged, the first fact was: Donald Trump won the election. That narrative expressed some mythic feeling these millions shared. That being (to them) beyond question, the Election Truther asks: what else had to have been true? Well, it must mean that the election was rigged, of course. Must have been. No other explanation fits. But who could have carried out such a huge trick? Well, the job would have been huuuuuuge, so it had to be an entity vast beyond comprehension. Thus does an image of "the Deep State" come into view and take shape: it fits the results the Deep State has produced as a key fits a lock. Ah, now it all makes sense.

The various components of the archetypal Truther Narrative protect its core message from any evidence that might undermine it. If THEY control all major sources of information, any such evidence has to be false. If THEY are capable of staging events that look like news, any particular thing we experience might not be real. THEY carry out false flag operations using agents they have planted among us, so when one of us begins to doubt the Truther Narrative, that's not a reason to think the theory might be false, it's a reason to think the doubter might not really be one-of-us.[3]

---

[3] Similar mechanisms play/played a part in the cult phenomenon.

Here, I should repeat for emphasis: I'm not saying that the Truther Narrative *is* a religion, only that it borrows certain features of religion to serve its own needs. Religion, at its best, situates the believer within a vast metaphorical understanding of the universe, opening him or her to a reality that surrounds, permeates, and stretches on beyond whatever experience offers at a given moment. Living in nothing more than the experience of a given moment makes life small. Living in the metaphor of a religious understanding of the universe makes life large. This is the essence of Christianity, of Islam, of Buddhism, of animist beliefs, of all religions. Science purports to arrive at true facts, religion at true meanings, where meaning consists of how the parts fit into some single whole, the more all-encompassing the better.

Truther Narrative may be *like* a religion, but it doesn't fit the description of religion I've just set forth because, instead of opening its devotees to a larger reality, it shrinks reality down to a script small enough for the believer to wear like a suit of form-fitting armor. Wherever a Truther Narrative grinds against experienced reality the believer can relieve the friction by shaving the irritating bit of reality away and moving it to the discard pile of falsehoods and irrelevancies that merit no attention.

The suit-of-armor analogy brings us to a crucial question. Why would people need or want the armor provided by Truther Narrative? What does it offer its believers? What does it protect them against? The list is long but here are a few items to consider:

- The Truther Narrative combats the intolerable idea that history is random. If it were, it would mean all of us are on a runaway train with no one in the control room. Truther Narrative tells the believer that someone *is* at the controls. It's not someone good but at least there's *someone.*
- The Truther Narrative explains free-floating anxiety that seems to have no specific cause. It tells believers their anxiety *does* have a cause: it's that evil unseen group behind the curtain--"but you," it tells the believer, "you're special: *you* have seen through the lie."
- The Truther Narrative suggests that something *can* be done about all the bad stuff happening: a human's doing all this, and a human can be stopped. If the Cabal is human, they're killable.
- The Truther Narrative offers relief for those who are feeling a hatred they cannot turn off. It gives them permission to hate without feeling like bad people. Wanting-to-hurt is what *good* people do, it tells them: in the face of an evil so vast, so apocalyptic it's only right to hate.
- Truther Narrative justifies a continuous anger that transcends this or that particular outrage. Of course you're angry all the time, Truther Narrative tells the believer: what the cabal is doing is inexcusable. You *should* be angry all the time.
- Truther Narrative tells believers they don't have to grope their way through a fog of moral ambiguity. It offers a

legible map of the moral universe, equipped with which the Conspiracy Theorist can tell right away if something is right or wrong, good or bad, true or false. It provides a fleeting taste of that exquisite balm that humans seek and rarely find: certainty.

How Narrative Works

Every narrative banks on our genetically embedded need to connect seemingly unrelated dots. Our survival depends on never turning off this mechanism, because only by connecting dots can we perceive whole pictures, and only by seeing whole pictures can we decipher the meanings of particular dots. A streak of yellow on a field of green is meaningless if it's just color and shape: why even notice it? As part of a whole scene, however, we might perceive that what we're seeing is the tail of a tiger moving toward us through the tall grass. We perceive it once we're seeing the whole picture because now it means something: now it's a discernable part of a single whole scenario that includes us and a tiger.

According to neural scientists, this is how all perception works.[4] The sense organs start the process of perception, but start-the-process is all they do. The sense organs browse the world gathering bits of data and sending them to the brain.

---

[4] I am not a scientist, neural or otherwise, My sources for these ideas include Jeff Hawkins and Sandra Blakeslee's *On Intelligence* (Times Books, 2004); Daniel Kahneman's *Thinking, Fast and Slow* (Farrar, Straus and Giroux, 2011); David Eagleman's *Incognito: The Secret Lives of the Brain* (Pantheon, 2011); Michael Chorost's *World Wide Mind* (Simon and Schuster); and Ransom Stephen's *The Left Brain Speaks, the Right Brain Laughs* (Viva, 2016).

The brain figures out how to fit each datum into a model it already contains--a model constructed from all previous experiences. As soon as it deciphers the "meaning" of each new bit of data, the brain plugs it into the model—situates the part within a whole. As soon as enough parts have been plugged in, the brain starts to predict what it's looking at. As soon as it guesses what it's looking at, the brain completes the perception with data supplied from memory. Only then do we see (hear/smell/feel/taste/whatever) that thing out there. And by then the brain has already sent messages to the motor nerves to do something about the thing out there.

If the prediction works, the model is confirmed and strengthened. If it fails, our brain amends the model as best it can to fit what seems to be out there. This, according to the latest decades of neural research, is what's happening constantly and ongoingly. It's happening at split-second speed, so we experience it as instantaneous: we look, we see. But actually, perception is a process. What we perceive out there is always, to some extent, a projection based on what we "know" to be out there, an internalized model we're constantly adjusting, based on incoming data.

When the brain is processing barrages of information (and when is it not?) it makes assumptions based on shortcuts. Something's getting bigger? Must mean it's coming closer. Sky is black? Must mean it's night. Sometimes, what's "obvious" isn't true, but the brain can't stop to check all or even most of its assumptions. Why? because the world never stops happening, and the brain has to keep up. Its job is to perceive patterns, and so it has to keep seeing patterns—whether they exist out there or not.

Assumptions that shape what we perceive as the world are mostly tacit, so we don't even know what is shaping those assumptions. When a researcher asked a roomful of people to answer the question: "How many of each kind of animal did Moses take on the Ark?" most people said two. The correct answer was zero: it wasn't Moses who took animals onto the Ark, it was Noah. Why did so many get it wrong?

Probably because, for anyone native to the Abrahamic tradition—Jews, Muslims, Christians—Moses, Noah, and the Ark are all part of the same narrative. All three raise the same ripple of associations. Cite any of those names and you've got Adam and Eve hovering in the background, and the Garden of Eden, and Satan, and maybe the Baptist church down the street, and maybe Pope Gregory the Great, depending on who you are. They're unstated, they're unnoticed but there they are: part of the picture that gives Moses and Noah and the Ark meaning.

Had the researcher asked, "How many of each kind of animal did LeBron James take onto the Ark?" most would have caught the error at once, because LeBron James stirs up a whole different constellation of unstated ideas: with him, suddenly NBA is in the air, and "take my talents to South Beach" and maybe Greatest of All Time and monster dunk. Depending on who one is, on what model one is carrying inside, these and other phantoms are in the air, unnoticed, shaping what one perceives.

Our Stories, Our Selves

All of which implies that *narrative* is part and parcel of perception. It's an essential element. Story is something we have a hard time *not* seeing because without it, we couldn't really see at all. Brotherton cites a famous study in which social psychologists showed a bunch of people a brief film of several geometric shapes moving about, and then asked them to describe what they'd seen. That was all they asked: what did you see? One subject said she saw a mother scolding her children, one saw a witch trapping hunters, one saw a big kid bullying little kids… they told different stories, but almost all reported what they'd seen in *terms* of story, even though they were given nothing but abstract shapes in motion. Apparently, that's just the kind of creature we are: the kind that perceives reality in terms of unfolding story: it's baked into our biology. Apparently this propensity gives us an evolutionary edge of some kind.

What could that edge be? Well, for one thing, by constructing narrative, we're connecting who we are to who we've been, which makes for a continuous self. I can see why that would be crucial. How could we function in the world without a continuous self? The very thought is frightening.

What's more, our instincts make us strive to see the same overall narrative framework as others of our social world—of our tribe, so to speak; since otherwise the tribe would drift in all directions and there would no longer *be* a tribe. A group narrative makes for a continuous *group*-self; and group-selves are no more eager to die than individual selves.

When a group of us have some single shared narrative framework, the words we use have the same meanings and implications for our cohorts as they do for us—given that the full meaning of any word reflects how it fits with the context in which it is used.[5] If everybody in a human group is living in a different perceived reality, they're not going to be able to make and carry out plans together in whatever reality is actually out there. We have, therefore, a continuous need (and therefore, a continuous impulse) to connect the dots, connect to the past, connect to others of our group, connect to what's around us: it's how we construct single whole worlds to be living in. And narrative is our single most indispensable mechanism for achieving all of this.

In short, all the traits associated with believing in Truther Narrative appear to be evolutionary survival traits. People especially drawn to Truther Narrative merely have a hyper-intense version of these traits. Take, for example, the trait most associated with spouters of Truther Narratives: spotting

---

[5] Educational psychologists generally hold that learning fundamentally *consists* of situating new bits of data within existing referential frameworks they call *schema*. I'm proposing here that schemas exist socially just as much as they do psychologically.

danger where none exists. At what point can this spotting-danger mechanism be identified as a disability? When exactly does hyper-vigilance cross the line into paranoia?

A medical expert might mention symptoms that can be objectively measured: pulse rate, perspiration, etc. And yes, we do picture people afflicted with paranoia as looking and acting a certain way: whispering furtively, glancing about constantly … The same sorts of images come to mind when we picture…well, Truther Narrative Nuts.

But outward signs such as these signify paranoia only when they don't match the context. The freaked-out furtive guy stands out if he's in a park on a Sunday afternoon among families having picnics. If we see the same fellow, behaving that same way, on a dark street in Damascus during the civil war with a building burning in the background and bullets whizzing past, his behavior is going to look normal. In that context, he'd seem weird to us if he were sitting calmly on a bench eating a sandwich and reading a comic book.

Context, then, is a crucial factor. Without taking context into account, we can't necessarily tell if someone is acting like a Truther Narrative Nut or like a normal person responding to a possibly real conspiracy. What's pertinent to mention now are those studies I mentioned earlier, about people finding hidden figures in pages of random scribble-scrabble. I said that people who believed in lots of Truther Narratives were apt to spot hidden images even when there were no hidden images to spot. In some versions of that study, researchers asked the subjects nothing about their belief in Truther Narratives. They focused directly on that underlying propensity to see hidden images. They were interested in finding out how the test conditions might affect that propensity.

So, for example, in one such study, the subjects were divided into two random groups. One group was taken to a neat room and asked to complete their assignment at well-ordered desks, with all the equipment they might need, right at hand. The other group was taken to a messy room and asked to do their work at desks piled high with junk, where they would have to clear a space for themselves amidst piles of detritus, while chaotic traffic passed through their work area, constantly and annoyingly interrupting them.

Who found more hidden figures? The results were clear: those who were doing their work amidst disorder. Apparently, chaos as a context intensified their need to find patterns among random data. Apparently, disorder in the environment sharpens a person's hunger for order. And apparently, finding hidden patterns where there are none feeds that hunger.

This experiment is one of many demonstrating the power of context to shape people's styles of decision-making and thus to shape what sorts of personalities neutral observers would judge them to be. To me, what this says is that, if there is such a thing as a personality type abnormally vulnerable to believing Truther Narratives, context can make any of us more like such a person or less like such a person. Context can put pressures on our narrative-generating mechanism that shape what that mechanism gets us to see and feel, and might distort the narrative it produces.

And yet, no matter what the context, that narrative-generating mechanism of ours keeps churning out a stream of narrative, keeps telling us who we are, what we've done, what we're in the middle of now, what's coming at us from out there, what to do about what's coming, and what to steer toward in a future that exists only in the big-picture story we see ourselves in, a future that might or might not come into being but which for all of us is all we have by which to navigate.

How Narratives Go Wrong

When we're forming a narrative by connecting dots, errors can creep in unnoticed. That's because the mechanisms of perception ensure that as a narrative is emerging, we're already straining to perceive what it is. As soon as we can, we're starting to supply from memory the dots that need to be there to complete the picture. That process might require seeing dots that aren't visible yet. The world we're living in is largely what our brain is constructing on the run, not a static replica of what's out there that our sense organs are picking up. As mentioned earlier, the world we live in is largely the one we "know" ourselves to be in. Therefore, we never actually *know* what's out there in the present moment. Not fully.

Not only that, but the world is full of stuff that we don't know we don't know. George Bush's defense secretary Donald Rumsfeld once said it's the unknown unknowns that'll getcha' and he was right. Mark Twain once said, it's not what you don't know that'll get you in trouble, it's what you know, that ain't true. He was right too. Most people think they know what a bicycle looks like, but when asked to complete a simple diagram of one, most people get it wrong. We think we know how a bicycle looks because we know how to work a bicycle; but those are two different things. The same goes for can openers, zippers, and cap-and-trade climate policy.

Every person has a headful of ideas they "know" to be true, drawn from experience, gleaned from rumors, vested in metaphors, hunches, and educated guesses...We don't check things we "know" for sure because we have to save our mental focus for things we're not sure about. No one looks for proof that the sky is blue because everyone *knows* it's blue. (Which it ain't, actually. Jes' sayin'...)

To compound this problem, all of us form opinions based on insufficient information. Some of us do more of this, some less, but we all do it, because evolution has rewarded us for it, has shaped us to behave this way. We form an opinion before all the evidence is in because all the evidence is *never* in. In *Suspicious Minds,* Brotherton reports an experiment in which people were asked whether they approved or disapproved of nanotechnology. Most had no opinion because (like me) they knew nothing whatsoever about nanotechnology. Then they were given two sentences of information about nanotechnology—two vague sentences that provided hardly any real information. After reading those sentences, a significant number of the people in the study had (like me) an opinion about nanotechnology, for or against.

That's how perception functions, that's how and why we construct narratives, and for the most part it works and it's useful. But, because of the way narrative works, when the social world becomes a landscape haunted by anxiety and uncertainty, Truther Narrative turns into something other than just another narrative. It turns into something more like a cancer cell. In a world haunted by ambiguity and uncertainty, a narrative that is something like a cancer cell has important advantages.

Here's why. A narrative is how we figure out what's really out there. We tell a story, we take action based on the assumption that our story is true, and if it works, we know our imagined picture of the world at least roughly matches the world that's actually out there, so we can safely take action based on that picture. In order to fulfill this function, however, a narrative must be flexible. The adjustments we are forced to make to reality are like our fingers touching against objects in a dark room as we grope about trying to make out shapes. If our narrative can't change in response to what we encounter, we have no way of knowing whether we're onto something or deluded. If our narrative is fixed by what we have inside and can't be changed by what's out there, we're like people moving through some lightless wilderness with a virtual-reality helmet strapped to our heads, so that we're always perceiving what's inside our head instead of what's out there. This is the trap into which the Truther Narrative draws believers.

The thing is, a healthy narrative can become non-functional if it's having to change so fast on so many fronts that it loses coherence. A narrative that's losing coherence is on its way to being dead and gone. This is when Truther Narrative has an edge over other narratives: it can remain unchanged in the face of contradictory evidence because, instead of changing in response to what's out there, Truther

Narrative changes (our perception of) what's out there in order to keep itself coherent.

It can do this because, built into the archetypal Truther Narrative are mechanisms for screening out information that might corrode the narrative and bring incoherence into its system. One such mechanism is the proposition that THEY control all mainstream sources of information. With this proviso, Truther Narrative can classify any information that tends to undermine it as false information coming from THEM. How does one tell if a new piece of information is true or false? One looks to see if it fits with all the things already "known to be true". For the believer, this filters out all information that might weaken whatever particular story the Truther Narrative is supporting and lets in any information that adds to the coherence of that story. The more coherence a narrative has, the more true it feels.

And there's more. According to the archetypal Truther Narrative, "THEY" can script and stage-manage huge events. What journalists report as "news" and what scholars later describe as "history" can be framed by Truther Narrative as part of the false story the evil cabal is telling. If one knows the cabal's story to be false, one can dismiss all the events the cabal is staging. In this way, the Truther Narrative can ensure that no actual event weakens any particular tale it's spinning. It can tell people swept up in some catastrophe—a bombing, a stock market crash, an epidemic, a weather emergency, a massive proliferation of hurricanes, wildfires raging out of control by the hundreds—

not to ask "What caused this?" but to ask instead, "Why did THEY do this? How does this serve THEIR plan?" This gives Truther Narrative a decided advantage because these are just the questions to which it has ready-made answers.

With such mechanisms, any given Truther Narrative can keep fortifying its internal consistency no matter what is said and no matter what happens. Internal consistency has the power to make a cluster of ideas feel true because each constituent idea feels true; and each of those feels true because it fits with every other idea in the cluster—each is the last piece of the puzzle needed to complete the big picture, which the Truther knows from the start to be true. And since each piece fits perfectly into that last remaining space, how could it not be true? Internal consistency gives a constellation of ideas social strength. A complex constellation full of nuance is vulnerable to erosion in times of stress, because when new information is coming in too rapidly to be absorbed, internal inconsistencies build up. This is why, in times of stress, Truther Narrative enjoys an enormous advantage over more open-ended narratives.

And let's not forget the proposition that THEY have placed agents among us, spreading lies. This clause gives a social group knit together by Truther Narrative a built-in way to expel members who are experiencing doubts or raising troublesome questions. It also provides a way to dismiss erstwhile insiders who embarrass the group by doing something the group needs to disavow. "It wasn't us who did this thing; it was one of them trying to make us look bad."

By keeping its binding narrative internally consistent, the community bound by that narrative is able to keep itself pure. And the purified community comes to value ever more sharply the exclusion of the polluting Other.[6]

There's one more way in which Truther Narrative is not just another narrative. It has a creepy ability to exploit other narratives in a parasitical way. It grows, one might say, by feeding on other narratives. That is, it can draw strands of those other narratives into its orbit as if by gravitational force, discarding the ones that don't fit, absorbing the ones that can be made to fit. Once incorporated into Truther Narrative, a strand of idea becomes part of a self-confirming non-falsifiable idea-cluster that resists erosion in the face of any and all contradictory evidence. That's the idea-cluster people are drawn to, if they're the type to be drawn into Truther Narrative.

---

[6] Mechanisms almost exactly similar to these can be discerned in the cult phenomenon.

The Virus Metaphor

Edgar Welch, the man at the center of the Pizzagate event, was arrested and sentenced to a four-year prison term for assault; but if we think of Pizzagate as the story of something Edgar Welch did, we end up focusing on that one guy, and we miss the big picture.

Because here's the thing. The Pizzagate phenomenon didn't originate with Edgar Welch, and it didn't end with him. It accumulated out of messages being published on a variety of websites and traded on social media. After the police took Welch away, the Pizzagate story kept spreading: it had a life of its own. By the end of that year, it had been shared an estimated 1.4 million times by 250,000 social media accounts.

In that process, the story accumulated details and grew horns. For example: having sex with babies gave the evil ones power, people were saying: this is why the elite were so into pedophilia. No one can identify exactly what people were saying this, and certainly no one can know what person said it first. After a while, the full-blown Pizzagate Truther Narrative was just there in the information cloud. In that way, a Truther Narrative is like a myth. It has no author. It emerges spontaneously out of the hubbub of many people telling one another what they've heard.

The website Info Wars run by Alex Jones reported some of the most lurid Pizzagate details in the language used for stories about heroes taking action. "We must protect the babies," Jones wrote. "One day it will be our family." But Jones and his associates were just tinkering and fiddling with stories that passed through their hands to others who tinkered and fiddled with them and passed them on to others. Like mythology, Truther Narratives are communally created.

Alex Jones and others spread the Pizzagate story, but they didn't *cause* it to spread. When you follow the whole trajectory of the Pizzagate story, you can't say anyone was *making* this happen. The story went viral because the underlying belief pool was already there and when the story dropped into those dank waters, it flourished like cholera. It was able to flourish in this context because here, in the ocean of what "people were saying", the story had complete freedom from the constraints of actual fact. It could live and feed on people's beliefs alone. When you look at the phenomenon as a whole, the word that pops is not paranoid but viral.

It's apt that the whole Pizzagate episode is commonly called a viral phenomenon, because when we look at the Truther Narrative—not this or that particular Truther Narrative but the social phenomenon as a whole—the virus metaphor seems a most apt description.

The idea that people who believe in Truther Narrative have certain identifiable personality traits, and that we all have these traits, implies that Truther Narrative is just part of the human condition. Brotherton says he wrote *Suspicion Minds* to make this very point: there are always strands of such stories floating about, and all of us are the sorts of people who might on a given day buy into them. Nothing to see here, move along—that was his implication.

I am not convinced. Yes, there might be odd bits of Truther Narrative floating about in most places at most times like dust bunnies in the corners of rooms where brooms can't easily reach. But Truther Narrative seems to flare more in some eras than in others. It seems to have more power in some places and periods than in others. Why would that be? This is where the virus metaphor shines a light.

Truther Narrative is more active in some periods/places than others because it is like an opportunistic infection. It lurks in the corners of the social universe until conditions are ripe and then it emerges to contaminate and spread.

And when are the conditions ripe? The virus metaphor again supplies an answer: when a society's immune system is weak. A healthy social universe is a web of interwoven narratives that forms an unstated but coherent whole, part of the collective subconscious of its inhabitants. In such a universe, countless open-ended narratives are nested in and amongst other narratives, and they're constantly in conversation with one another, overlapping and interacting as they adjust to one another and to real events.

The fabric woven of these many narratives is a meta-narrative too big for insiders to see, because it is what gives those insiders the eyes with which they see, and one thing no eye can see is itself seeing. That interwoven web of narratives does, however, constitute a frame of reference by which everyone can be setting their own individual and group agendas without totally messing up everyone else's. A society's immune system, I venture to suggest, is the coherence of the whole web of narratives that permeates a functional society.

As animals we live in geography, but as humans, we live in a social universe made up entirely of narratives. That's the landscape in which a Truther Narrative can come alive as something other than just-another-narrative. When traces of incoherence begin to show, viral specks of Truther Narrative move out of hiding and begin to attack the body of a culture as a whole—by worming their way into the narratives of the culture. Truther Narrative has mechanisms that allow it to find and enter host narratives and hijack them, just as a virus enters a host cell, hijacks its DNA, and uses that to make copies of itself: in a landscape comprised of narratives not cells and organisms, this is how Truther Narrative replicates itself and spreads.

Hosts can be narratives of various sorts found in most social landscapes: any theory, arguable or otherwise, about actual people plotting to do bad things in the real world is open to infection. Host narratives of this description abound because people frequently *do* collude to commit nefarious deeds, do forge unsavory plots, which sometimes come to light and sometimes don't. Any time a theory about such a plot gets articulated, Truther Narrative sniffs an opportunity and moves in. If it can get inside the theory, it can corrupt the reasonable, arguable, debatable proposition into a version of itself.

Take the fate of physicist Stephen Jones, for example, one of the founders of the "9/11 Truther" movement. He started out arguing that the collapse of Building Seven, one of the buildings in the World Trade Center, was a case of controlled demolition, and he offered physical data to back up his theory. He was a physicist and the kind of data he presented was the kind that a physicist is qualified to present. I'm not saying his theory was correct, I'm only saying that in the beginning he put concrete data on the table where it could be studied by others and tested to see if the claim held up. That's what goes on in any debate among humans about what's true and what's not, and that debate is not just okay but indispensable. That's what the social thinking process amounts to: it's a living web of ongoing conversations about what's true and what isn't.

Stephen Jones's theory was, however, close enough to Truther Narrative to come within its gravitational field. Strands of Truther Narrative began to infest it. And then more strands found their way in. And today, Stephen Jones himself is a Sandy Hook denier and claims the Holocaust, the attempted genocide of the Jews by Nazi Germany, was a hoax. His theory, it would seem, came close enough to a

Truther Narrative to get hijacked, and now he is occupied by that body snatcher.[7]

Truther Narrative exploits structures already in our psyches and sucks juice from myths already embedded in our culture. The 4000-year-old story of Gilgamesh and Humbaba, the 1200-year-old story of Beowulf and Grendel's Mother, the forty-year-old story of Luke Skywalker and Darth Vader, the 30-year-old story of Harry Potter and Voldemort—each of these stories emerged in a particular cultural context, each is full of details that have resonance particular to its own time and place of creation; yet they all share a certain underlying, archetypal structure. And because of that underlying archetypal structure, each one, despite differences in detail, activates a music in the psyches of those among us who grew up with that story. In itself, I would call this a good thing. Children absorb tribal myths and unshakeable beliefs out of stories they hear as they're first coming into language, myths that help to give them their two most precious human possessions: self-hood and membership. Any society in which every member has both of these things is likely to be a healthy and well-functioning society. The myths of a culture are the healthy cells of its self-hood.

That's just the kind of story Truther Narrative can infect, the way a virus infects a healthy cell: the virus then uses the

---

[7] Whether Jones entertained ideas of this kind all along, I don't know; but if he did, he kept it to himself as far as I know.

DNA of the formerly healthy cell to replicate itself. That's why Alex Jones started his Info Wars shows with the theme from Star Wars, and that's how David Icke could convince a remarkable number of people that seven-foot mind-controlling lizard-like aliens called Archons were actually in control of Earth, feeding on the emotions generated by traumatized humans, a conspiracy so vast that only he could see it—until he started telling it and then people who entertained vaguely similar stories began to see it too. And that's also why some people can believe the Earth is flat.

And it matters that context is a key factor in whether any given individual is vulnerable to the Truther virus, because every one of us as individuals has a context every minute of every day. We're part of a certain family, which is part of some larger group of people, who have a history. Our local context is nested in bigger contexts, which are nested in even bigger contexts. We're living in a certain neighborhood, a certain city, a certain country, among certain sorts of people, doing some certain form of work, socializing with certain others in certain ways typical of people like us. We're living in a particular period of time—the digital age, the year of the pandemic, our early twenties, the 21st century—whatever. Many different contexts are operating on our sensibilities at any given moment and what they are vary from person to person, but one thing is for sure: no one exists in isolation from context, and no one is separable from his or her context.

The biggest context of all is history. If the virus metaphor holds water, we should see some evidence of it by looking at the Truther Narrative phenomenon in various historical settings, for history is the river in which all of us are floating. Or swimming as the case may be. Or drowning. If context is a critical factor in the ebb and flow of Truther Narrative, then we should find that Truther Narrative is not a constant presence crashing around breaking furniture everywhere in history. Instead, we should find that, in some periods and places, it has been a fringe phenomenon touted by eccentrics on the margins of society and in other periods and places it has spiked, found volatile exponents, and/or spread from person to person to manifest as movements. If such turns out to be the case, it would be useful, surely, to examine what those periods and places have in common, because it does seem like we might be in one of those periods now.

Part Two
The Truther Narrative
in History

14th Century:
Two Protypes Are Born

Decades ago, when I first started looking into the history of Truther Narrative, one historical time and place caught my eye immediately: Western Europe in the 14th century. In this place, in this era, *two* prototypical Truther Narratives were born within a few decades of each other—separate stories that arose in different locales but had eerie similarities. Not only were their shared features suggestive but elements of both stories have been turning up in Truther Narratives ever since and are discernable in new Truther Narratives churning to the surface even today.

The first of these two 14th century narratives gave frightful expression to the ideas and attitudes known as Anti-Semitism. All over the world, don't we still hear, "The Jews are behind it" about all sorts of random catastrophic events. In the aftermath of 9/11, (false) rumors immediately rippled up that Jews working in the Twin Towers had inexplicably received instructions to stay home that day.

The other of these two 14th century Truther Narratives, which I am calling prototypical, fielded the idea that a powerful, evil, secret society is operating behind the scenes of everyday life—a "Deep State", you might say. In the pages ahead, I will refer to this one as the secret-society template of Truther Narrative.

The Jewish Moneylender

The first of these two prototypical stories came out of a cluster of events that took place in England in the 1290s, involving Jewish moneylenders, Christian peasants, English lords, and two kings named Henry III and Edward I.

It's important to note, however, that the soil for this Truther Narrative began to form much earlier. It began to form in the early days of the Roman empire, back when Christianity first branched away from Judaism to become a separate religion. In those first few centuries, both faiths went through periods of intense persecution by the Roman state. Then in the 4th century, Christians took over the Roman world and *became* the Roman state. Christianity was declared the state religion at that point, and all forms of pagan worship were outlawed.

Jews, however, posed a doctrinal problem. They weren't pagans—but they weren't Christians either, though the two shared an ancestral parent. What emerged was a complex doctrine, set forth explicitly by John Chrysostom, the archbishop of Constantinople—and Constantinople being the capital of the Roman world at that point, his word was as close to law as could be.

Chrysostom declared that God had chosen the Jewish tribe to herald the end of time. One day, all the Jews would accept Christ as their savior en masse. On that day, Christ would return to Earth, and the Day of Judgment would be at hand. Christians had a duty to protect Jews, to ensure that they would be around to play their pivotal role when the apocalyptic moment came.

On the other hand, Chrysostom declared, it was the Jews who killed Christ. So until that time, they must not be allowed to challenge Christian hegemony or acquire any share of power. Chrysostom's doctrine spawned laws barring Jews from owning land, wielding weapons, or joining armies. In the Dark Ages that followed the collapse of Roman order, the economy of Europe was based almost entirely on land and military might. In that world, everybody was either a peasant, a feudal lord, or a functionary of the Church. Within European Christendom, there were no pagans or Muslims (nor, of course, Hindus, Buddhist, Shintoists, etc.) Everybody in this realm was Christian except for the Jews—whom Christians were duty-bound to protect from extinction but exclude from any form of power.

Jews became, therefore, the personification of the Other in Europe. They were few in number, but they were scattered throughout the realm. Excluded from the mainstream economy, they made their living as best they could, mostly as itinerant peddlers, traveling from village to village selling trinkets and household sundries.

Then the dominant culture did find a use for Jews after all. Christians weren't allowed to charge interest on loans to other Christians—any interest at all was labeled usury, and it was a big no-no. But if no one can profit from lending money, no one will lend money; and every society of even a little complexity needs at least a little lending to take place sometimes.

Jews, as it happens, were under the same restriction as Christians: their religious laws forbade them to charge interest on loans to other Jews. But Jews could lend money at interest to Christians and Christians to Jews. Moneylending didn't emerge as a profession among Christians because there was hardly anybody they could lend to. It emerged as a profession among Jews because their potential customer base included almost everybody in Christendom.

Early on, Jewish moneylenders probably did most of their lending to peasants, because that's who most people were. Nobody used money much in that barter-based economy, but when they did, it was usually for some life crisis. If a peasant needed to borrow money, it meant they had run into some really bad moment in their life story. If a Jewish moneylender turned up as a character in stories circulating among peasants, he probably wouldn't be a jolly fellow everybody was glad to see.

By the time the Crusades got underway, Europe had started to emerge from the feudalism of medieval times. By the high middle ages, duchies and lordships and counties and even kingdoms were forming. The people who needed big-time money were increasingly king-like figures—Lords with Swords, let's call them. I capitalize the words to make this a term for a certain kind of figure who emerges in every society even after they're no longer called lords and no longer wield physical swords.

The Lords with Swords of this period frequently needed money to fight battles. There was only so much they could get by wringing more taxes from their peasants without causing such resentment that they risked driving their peasants into rebellion, which was dangerous because the peasants were numerous. But as long as there were some Jews around, there was another way for Lords with Swords to get money. In a crunch, they could get it from Jewish moneylenders. So Lords with Swords began to license selected Jews to operate as moneylenders in areas they controlled, in exchange for a licensing fee.

Income from these fees was one benefit a feudal nobleman could derive from having a Jewish moneylender of his own—but not the only one. When he needed sudden money, he could borrow it from "his" Jew, or he could just seize all "his" Jew's gold as a punishment for usury. The possessive pronoun is deliberate here, for the lords of feudal Europe did see Jewish moneylenders as assets that could be possessed. They bought and sold "their" Jews to one another from time to time and didn't balk at using the language of bought-and-sold to describe these transactions. What was bought and sold was the right to tax, borrow from, or fine those particular Jews.

If a fine was imposed on him, the Jew would have to call in loans made to peasants and poor people. This aroused resentment, but it wasn't directed at the lord, for he wasn't the one asking for money. It was the Jew demanding money, it was he who became the bad guy. This pattern of relationships was not a Truther Narrative. It was simply the social order of medieval Europe when the Crusades began: the system familiar to all. Like it or hate it, you had to live with it: this was how the world worked. This was, however, the soil in which a Truther Narrative began to germinate, as the last of the Crusades were winding down.

The first traces of this Truther Narrative came out of a creepy event that happened in a town called Norwich when a little boy named William was found dead. His mother dreamed that local Jews had murdered him. A man named Thomas of Monmouth wrote something like a true-crime book titled *The Life and Miracles of St. William of Norwich* in which he claimed that William was killed by Jews as part of an annual ritual called "Passover". Every year, said Monmouth, Jews killed a Christian boy and used his blood in their ritual. Most people were illiterate, but the few who read Monmouth's story told it to the many who couldn't read, and so the story spread in viral form. Over the next hundred-plus years, it sparked sporadic outbursts of mob violence against Jews.

Then came the game changer. Another boy was murdered—or at least, he was found dead in a well owned by a Jew, in the town of Lincolnshire. As it happened, two prominent Jewish families were celebrating a wedding in Lincolnshire just then, and guests had gathered from far and wide.

As it also happened, Henry the Third, king of England, who had previously "owned" the Jews of Lincolnshire had just recently "sold" them to his brother—but the contract had one proviso: if any Lincolnshire Jews were convicted of a crime, the king would retain possession of those Jews without having to give back the money he'd received from his brother.

The king sent an investigator to Lincolnshire to look into the death of "little St. Hugh." The investigator tortured the well-owner into confessing that the Jews had not actually gathered in Lincolnshire for a wedding but to pick a victim for their Passover ritual and had chosen Little Saint Hugh. King Henry endorsed the verdict.

His endorsement ensured that the Jews of Lincolnshire were found guilty. Seventy-nine Lincolnshire Jews were executed, their wealth reverted to the king, and a wave of pogroms broke out across England, during which Lords with Swords all across the land repudiated their debts to Jewish moneylenders. In 1290, Henry's successor, King Edward I, issued a decree expelling all Jews from England. Most moved to the continent, which was fine with the English aristocracy because they no longer needed Jewish moneylenders: the Church's hold had broken enough by this time that there were now lots of Christians to borrow from in Europe: in Amsterdam, in Lombardy, even in London.

These events marked an ominous turn for anti-Semitism, but the Truther Narrative wasn't a developed story yet. It was mostly a diffuse feeling among peasants, egged on by Lords with Swords. One might suppose that after all the Jews had been expelled, stories about Jews would fade away in England. But that's not what happened. With all the real Jews gone, *stories* about Jews (told not as stories but as "news" of real events) were free to evolve in any direction the narrative needed them to go. Nothing people said would now be contradicted by actual experience since few were likely to meet any actual living, breathing Jews in England now. If the culture was looking for a certain sort of story, there was nothing to stop the Jewish Moneylender from becoming the character the story needed to become a "better" story.

From the point of view of narrative, it wasn't enough that he be malicious. He had to be evil. The attractions of the story included the shivers it aroused, and "evil" raised better shivers than mere "malice". From the point of view of narrative, he couldn't just be powerful. It made for a better story if he was immensely and mysteriously powerful. His very absence could serve the story. In the story, his absence could be a ruse. Now he could still be around, behind some curtain, pulling strings. In his absence, people could now wonder how the Jew got so rich in the first place. Jews didn't farm, the king repeatedly seized their ill-gotten gold, and yet somehow they popped up again just as rich as before, lending out money and collecting their evil interest. Was Satan involved? The expulsion of the Jews left worms of story such as these wriggling around in English culture, available to storytellers weaving tales of conspiracy.

The Knights Templars

The other striking Truther Narrative that formed in this period emerged in France and it didn't center on Jews. Instead, it zeroed in on the most Christian of Christians. It was built around a monastic military order called the Knights Templar.

It began with a dramatic event that occurred on February 13, 1307. On that Friday, France's King Phillip ordered his constables to fan out across the land and arrest all members of the Knights Templar. Six hundred Templars were arrested that day, as well as thousands of people working for them. The ensuing trials dragged on for years. During that time, the Templar order was disbanded by the Pope and outlawed in France. When the trials finally ended, it was because there were no more Templars to put on trial. That much is fact.

As story, however, the Knights Templar were not gone. As story, in fact, they're still around. They crop up in popular American entertainments such as the Indiana Jones movies, and *The Da Vinci Code*. Somehow, they make for good fiction. That's how everyone I know takes it when the Templars turn up in some movie or TV show today.

But the Templars really did exist; and around them, in the 14th century, traces of a prototypical Truther Narrative did form. Who were those original Templars? Why did the King of France and the Pope of Christendom collude to wipe them out?

Let's start with some background. In the 10th century or so, a popular pilgrimage movement swelled in Europe. People began picking their way east to visit Christian shrines in the Holy Land in hopes of increasing their chances of salvation. But the road was long and difficult, and money was an issue. You had to carry along enough to pay your way there and back, but local currency didn't work as soon as you got any distance from home. The money you carried had to be in a form that was universally negotiable. Gold and silver were best.

But the roads were infested with ruffians looking for just that kind of money. Pilgrims traveled as groups, but marauders hit them anyway. Some hired bodyguards, but they couldn't be sure the bodyguards wouldn't kill them. Then Muslim Turks conquered the Holy Land, the Crusades began, and now pilgrims had to not just fend off marauders but make their way through battle zones to reach the sacred landscapes.

In 1119, a French knight decided to do something about all this. He gathered a bunch of his fellow knights, they took vows of poverty as monks, and made it their mission to help pilgrims travel safely to Palestine and back. The Pope exempted them from taxation and gave them permission to commit violence without incurring sin. They called themselves the Poor Soldiers of Christ, but everyone soon came to know them as the Knights Templar, because they made the Temple of Soloman their headquarters in the east.

The Templars were instantly among the celebrated elite of feudal European society, the very face of Christian triumph. Early on, they garnered a heroic reputation as warriors. Once, people said, the Templars helped a force of about 500 knights rout an army of 26,000 Muslims. The stuff of legends!

In the course of the Crusades, however, European Christians built three kingdoms in the heart of the Holy Land, whereupon commerce began to flow between Western Europe and Palestine. Soon there were people who didn't want to *travel* to Palestine, they just wanted to move money back and forth for commercial reasons.

The Templars were well set up to serve this need. They morphed into something like a Western Union of their time. In fact, they transported so much money back and forth that they outgrew the need to transport any physical form of money at all. Piles of gold, silver, and locally negotiable currencies accumulated at each end, and when someone wanted to send some money, the Templars could simply add the deposited value to the pile at one end and subtract the same amount from the pile at the other end. Nothing needed to travel but information: how much and to whom. Numbers and words. There was nothing for marauders to hijack.

The Poor Soldiers of Christ had sworn to live an impoverished lifestyle, and I'm not saying they abandoned their vows. Maybe they still lived on bread and water as individuals, but the Templars as an order began to get very rich, because they had learned something from all the money-handling they were doing. They'd found ways to turn a profit from lending money.

It might seem odd that the Templars could get rich this way, because they were the Christians' Christians, and on the question of "usury" the Church remained adamant: good Christians did not lend money at interest to fellow Christians.

But here's the thing. Lending money at interest was strictly forbidden in the Muslim world too. Muslim society, however, was boomingly commercial. In fact, commerce had been of the essence in Islam from the start, for the Prophet Mohammed himself was involved in commerce: he was a caravan leader for a wealthy merchant whom he eventually married. In the Islamic world, the best minds of the age had been busy for centuries working out ways to operate around the prohibition on interest. Muslims had developed countless ingenious mechanisms to facilitate lending such as charging a use fee instead of interest: you were not *lending* the money; you were *renting it out*, was the idea. By the time the Knights Templars arrived on the scene, the Muslims had it down to a science.

The Templars absorbed the inner workings of this science because when they weren't *fighting* the Muslims of the Holy Land, they were doing business with them. They morphed into big-time landowners because they were no longer just helping poor pilgrims get to the Holy Land and back, they were lending money to dukes and kings who needed it for armies and roads and thrones and pomp and infrastructure.

The Templars had started out as legendary heroes of the epic Christian cause, but by the 14th century, whispers were circulating that they were the agents of a secretive, evil cult based in the Islamic world known as the "Assassins." How could this be?

The answer is obvious: they were still the face of the Crusades, but the Crusades were now going poorly. European Christians had lost Jerusalem to the Muslims. Christians were regularly fighting amongst themselves. The Templars' victories had come early, their ignominious defeats were piling up late. Once, it was said, they sallied into the desert to battle Muslims and forgot to bring any water. They all died of thirst. They were an embarrassment to Christianity. In the 1290s, when the Templars lost their last stronghold in the east, they became a perfect metaphor for the failure of the epic Christian cause.

All this was happening just as the Templars were becoming a formidable force in European politics, a power they were gaining not from military prowess or piety but from their mastery of money. They were bending lords and bishops to their will because they knew how to make money on loans.

In 1307, King Phillip of France found himself deeply in debt to the Templars. He couldn't pay his debts by raising taxes on the peasants—he was already squeezing them to the near-breaking point. So he decided to cancel his debt by arresting the Templars for heresy and confiscating all their gold. He figured a lot of powerful people would support this move because lots of them owed money to the Templars too. Just to be on the safe side, though, he consulted the pope, and hallelujah: . the pope saw the wisdom of his plan (he owed the Templars too).

King Phillip and Pope Clement drew up a list of charges, none of which mentioned money. The charges focused on religious morality, on the Muslim enemy, and on sexual depravities. They sound suspiciously like the charges spouted in modern times, on websites such as Alex Jones's Info Wars, against the so called 'liberal elite'. The Templars were charged with over a hundred lurid sins all in all. They included:

- requiring initiates to deny that Christ was the son of God;
- requiring initiates to spit three times on the cross;
- requiring member of the order to drink a beverage made of the ashes of dead Templars;
- requiring members to have sex with other Templars;
- requiring members to kiss the Grand Master's ass— yes, literally. His anus.
- engaging in orgies with women just so they could consume the babies born of these sex riots, and…worst of all—

- worshipping a horned demon with the legs and head of a goat and the breasts of a woman. This demon was named Baphomet.

Baphomet was a corruption of two words associated with Islam: Mohammed, the prophet of Islam; and Baba, a standard title for the head of a Sufi brotherhood.[8] Conflating Baba and Mohammed into Baphomet added a Muslim-flavored odor of black magic to the Templars. Adding Baphomet-worship to the indictments let the King link the Templars to sundry troubles besetting common folks, because now, evil magic was involved. A church caught fire? A farmer couldn't get his wife pregnant? His cows died? A bridge collapsed? Could have been those Baphomet-worshipping Templars using supernatural help to make bad things happen.

As I mentioned, there wasn't just one Templars trial but many. The Grand Master of the order Jacques De Molay was burned at the stake in 1310, along with his deputy, but the trials went on, as lesser ex-Templars were located and hauled before various local tribunals to answer for the harms they'd caused. You can see how such a sensational ongoing legal

---

[8] A Sufi brotherhood is a type of Islamic religious order. It's somewhat analogous to a monastic order. The word Baba simply means "Father", so addressing the head of a Sufi brotherhood as Baba would be like addressing the head of a monastic order as "Father".

drama might have permeated talk in the taverns and shaped opinion in the streets, as people re-hashed the arguments made in court. Imagine if the OJ Simpson trial had last eleven years and had been happening in many towns across the country, not just L.A.

Once there were no more Templars to be found, the Truther Narrative spawned by the Templar's drama was free to take off and evolve. Whatever their motives, the King and the Pope had planted among the people an idea with survival power: that a small, evil group with access to supernatural forces, was making all the bad things happen. The King and the Pope wanted credit for identifying the group and wiping it out, but if the Templars were gone, the question could not help but arise: how come terrible things were still happening?

There were two possible explanations. One, the king and the pope were wrong or lying. That opened the door to disturbing thoughts. If the Pope, especially, was wrong or lying, could the Church itself be wrong or lying? Much less disturbing was another explanation. The Templars weren't really gone. That would be scary, of course, but it wouldn't shake the foundations of reality. The church would still be the church. The overarching narrative in place for centuries would still be true. The world was already known to be full of scary bad-guys. Adding one more group of scary bad guys to the picture wouldn't really change the big picture. It would at least suggest that something tangible could be done about the problems: the bad guys could be found and stopped.

This, then, was the soil in which the seeds of a Knights Templar Truther Narrative began to germinate. Stories accumulated about the "mystery" of the Templars' gold, for instance. The Templars having been so rich, they must have had mountains of the stuff. So what happened to it all? Rumor had it that when the king's constables burst into the Templars' offices, all they found were dusty books filled with numbers. Where did the gold go?

Stories circulated about a wagon that had left Paris the day before the arrests. How suspicious was that?! Others said, forget the wagon, the wagon was just a red herring to distract simpletons; on the day in question a mysterious *ship* left the harbor. A whole *shipload* of gold! That was a better fit for the story forming about these Templars: a mysterious group with powers so frightful they could make the crops wither and thanks to their Baphomet monster, inflict any kind of harm.

No Templars to be seen? Well, of course not. They were operating from hidden headquarters, people were saying. Under a new name, people were saying. You wouldn't know you were looking at one if you saw him on the street—they looked just like anyone now, people were saying. With their boundless wealth, Templars would have no trouble staying hidden. If it required building a whole secret city under Paris, they'd have the money to do it. After all, their descendants built a secret headquarters under the Denver International airport. Just a theory but it sure would explain a lot.

What the Similarities Suggest

Despite their differences, these two Truther Narratives had certain striking similarities. First of all, there were three key elements at play in both cases: Lords with Swords, Peasants with Grievances, and a conspicuous minority convenient for scapegoating. Both began as folkloric rumors circulating among peasants. In both cases, as rumors interwove with rumors, a narrative structure formed, to which further rumors could attach, until a story was forming. Then too, there was a functional similarity. In both cases, the Truther Narrative redirected the resentments of Peasants-with-Grievances away from the most obvious target, Lords-with-Swords, and toward a scapegoated minority.

In both cases, the group targeted for scapegoating was one with a history of exposure to diversity that set them apart from the mainstream culture of their society. In medieval times, European peasants rarely went far from home. They lived in small, monocultural communities, they had no newspapers or mass media of any kind, and their sense of the world congealed out of personal interactions with other locals. Jews couldn't own land, so they weren't part of that rural scene. Moving from village to village as itinerant peddlers, they surely couldn't help but notice that people in different places had somewhat different values, ideas, and concerns.

At the same time, their experience rendered them notably insular. When they came to a new village or town, they went wherever other Jews lived. Of course they did, since they were sure to feel so much more at home in the Jewish quarter; but it did allow non-Jews to wonder what secrets those Jews might be whispering among themselves in those ghettoes of theirs.

And the Templars? Well, they too had seen other lands and cultures. They'd walked where people were babbling in countless languages. And when they got back to monocultural Europe, they might well have felt more comfortable in conversation with other Templars than with the common herd, because some of the things that came out of a Templar's mouth might have sounded like heresy to peasants; and in the Europe of this era heresy was as serious as a heart attack, so to speak, for during the late Crusades, the Church had launched an investigative procedure called the Inquisition whose mandate was to search out heretics and purify them or put them to death. In that context, people weren't going to feel comfortable saying things in public that might sound even a little bit heretical.

The two prototypes had another singular point in common. Both emerged at a time when the nature of money was going through a drastic change, and both involved a group that was ahead of the curve on this change. It wasn't a rich/poor thing; it had to do with abstraction. To an ordinary peasant, wealth was something tangible, something one could see and touch. It was easy to understand why a rich guy was rich: he had land and he had the armed might to make others work that land for him. His wealth and power might have felt unjust, but it wasn't incomprehensible.

In the early Dark Ages, even coins had been something of an abstraction in Europe. You can't eat a coin or wear a coin, you can only trade it for something you can eat or wear, and if there was nothing to trade for, coins would not mean much. During the early Dark Ages, there wasn't much to trade for in Europe.

By the time the Crusades were underway, crossroads markets had formed and trade fairs were beginning to sprout here and there. As trade burgeoned, coins meant more and more.

They had to, because coins held the commercial world together. Even coins had a level of abstraction built into them. They ultimately represented a belief about what other people believed. That is the crucial point about any form of money. It's not enough to think that some form of money has value. If other people don't think it has value, then it doesn't.

Sharing beliefs about vital matters with other people is one of the main connecting tissues of a society. To accept any form of money is to participate in a system of interactive belief. But even if coins are one level of abstraction above barter, they're at least hard and shiny and if you put two in your pocket, you can hear them clinking, so it isn't *that* hard to believe a coin has "real" value. Even in a world of barter, peasants could trust that if they accepted a coin for something of tangible value, they could trade it to someone else for something of tangible value.

By the 14th century, however, when these two prototype Truther Narratives were emerging, something new was happening to money. Accounting information was joining coins as a functional form of money. The Jewish moneylenders and the Knights Templar were among the first in Christendom to pioneer an understanding of money in this new way.

When money became a form of information, as it did in the moneylending trade, it jumped to a higher level of abstraction. It was hard for the peasant-in-the-field to fathom this new kind of money, what it was, how to get some, how to use it. In 14th century Europe, the Jewish moneylenders and the Templars were both getting comfortable with money that existed purely as accounting-information. This was great for them—until Truther Narrative began looking for a scapegoat, at which point this kind of expertise attracted the wrong kind of notice.

Then there's a third crucial similarity between these two prototypes. Both cut through complexity to explain a lot, at a time when there was a lot in need of explanation. For one thing, this was a period of exceptional dislocation and hubbub. The Crusades, the great unifying project of Christendom, had finally, definitively failed in the east. Men with military skills were coming back, and at home, they were coalescing into gangs for hire—free-lance companies, they were called. An over-abundance of fighters needing employment meant there had to be wars in which freelance companies could fight.

Wars waged for no fundamental reason except that there were warriors were inevitably going to feel meaningless. Constant meaningless violence made the future unpredictable. The more unpredictable the future is, the more meaningless does planning for it feel. It didn't help that successive years of catastrophically heavy rainfall early in the 14th century led to years of bad harvest—this, just as Lords with Swords in England and France were mounting military campaigns that required raising taxes—on peasants. Sudden, unusual weather events had always triggered superstitious explanations, especially in agricultural societies where so much vital planning is based on expectations about the weather in the upcoming seasons. The 14th century was no exception.

But there was more, much more. In fact, the sheer quantity of social change was contributing mightily to malaise. Everywhere one looked in this era, people were on the move—after centuries when hardly anyone went anywhere. There were new roads, and on those roads, highwaymen were having a field day. People were flowing into growing cities, where crime was said to flourish in the markets and back alleys. And then came the Black Death, and in those burgeoning cities, corpses piled up so fast, no one could keep up with even burying them.

The Black Death wiped out a third or more of all Europeans—to be followed by radically inexplicable events such as women taking charge of lands and businesses owned by menfolk who had died. Social progress we would call it now, looking back, but at the time? Women running businesses? Women giving orders? This wasn't the way things were supposed to be!

What's more, with so many peasants having died, the remaining few enjoyed unprecedented bargaining power and could walk away from the land if they chose. Unprecedented! If serfs could simply walk away from the land, who else might walk away from what? And then, there were episodes of peasants attacking castles and burning down manor houses. Things like that weren't supposed to happen! It was like cows suddenly giving birth to two-headed calves. Peasant uprisings must have felt like they violated nature, even to the peasants rising up. If things like that could happen, what *couldn't* happen?

And what about these merchants one was starting to see, strutting about like earls? It didn't make sense. Merchants didn't own vast tracts of land, they didn't have bands of loyal sword-swinging vassals around them. How could merchants be wielding such power suddenly?

Historian Barbara Tuchman called this era "the catastrophic 14th century." To my mind, catastrophe is not the most notable point to zero in on here. Something bigger than calamity was happening in this period and it had to do with change itself. It wasn't that this thing or that thing was changing. The change was systemic, the change was global. The change was so top-to-bottom, horizon-to-horizon that the world itself was losing definition. Some new world was materializing, and no one could see what it was yet.

If you think of European history as the life-story of a culture, this late medieval period must be considered one of its pivotal chapters. Driving this vast transformation was a question that no longer seemed to have a clear answer: how was one to know what was true? The assumption had always been: if the question is important, the Church will know. This applied not just to spiritual matters but to material questions too, because the Church had proved its material might by building cathedrals, managing land, collecting taxes, spending money, calling armies into existence, and fighting wars.

So when the Black Death arrived, consider how the world must have felt. Everywhere one looked, people were dropping dead, and death by any of the three forms of plague was particularly horrible. Now as never before, the Church was called upon to deliver on its promises. Tell us, Church: what should we do now? About the Black Death, the Church had nothing to offer but prayers, rituals, confession, and self-flagellation, none of which worked one single bit.[9]

---

[9] The early 14th century, it's worth noting, was also when the Witch Craze took off in Europe. Over the next two centuries, between 200,000 and 750,000 people, mostly elderly widowed or unmarried women, were burned at the stake as witches: the Inquisition accused them of being agents of Satan pretending to be ordinary humans. The same social conditions that fed the Truther Narratives fed this horrific movement too.

In this context, a cunning figure hidden behind a curtain fit right into the emerging story. A hidden figure using gold and Satan to manipulate the world would explain a lot. Any story that explained a lot was going to have some traction in a world where there was such a lot in need of explanation. The Moneylending Jew, a supernatural power, secretly wreaking havoc? The Templars, operating from secret headquarters, deploying their monstrous Baphomet? Ah, now it all made sense. Sing on, blind muse!

Social Paradigm

What can we conclude about Truther Narrative from looking at this historical setting—Western Europe in the aftermath of the Crusades? When I add it up, I'm ready to hypothesize the following. Truther Narratives flare when the social paradigm is changing. What do I mean by social paradigm? Let me put it this way: think of society as a collectively-woven web of narratives and beliefs. In "stable" times, "normal" times, everyone is pretty familiar with the overall web. They might disagree with this or that person about this or that strand, but they know where they and others stand within the web as a whole. In stable times, they can predict how this whole tableau will look tomorrow. An interwoven four-dimensional web of this type is what I'm calling a social paradigm.[10]

The term paradigm comes from the philosophy of science. There, it refers to a broad theory that explains the various phenomena people observe within a given scientific field. The normal work of scientists consists largely of filling in the gaps in the theory and accounting for anomalies—bits of observed data that don't quite seem to fit.

I'm using *social* paradigm to mean the broad network of understandings and ideas that knit a whole society together. Such a network functions, as a paradigm does in science, to identify the everyday work that must be done right now (and, more generally, must be done "these days"), the problems and contradictions in need of remedy, and the methods and mechanisms by which these remedies might be achieved.

In science such adjustments ensure that the paradigm continues to provide a reliably accurate description of the real world. In social life, a paradigm ensures that people can go about their daily business confident that other people will behave more or less as one expects. If one is driving north toward an intersection and the light is green, one assumes that people driving east or west have a red light and will

---

[10] Metanarrative is another term often used for this concept; to me, however, *metanarrative* feels more like a word for the shell that contains a system—what you'd see if you were outside the system, seeing it as a whole. Here, I prefer social paradigm, because it feels more like something that permeates an entire system, that's in every part of it without being visible in any part of it.

know to stop. That's a simple and very material example. More nuanced examples would involve, say, needing to borrow money from a neighbor; or initiating an exchange intended to end in a sexual tryst; or persuading strangers to join a business enterprise, or sounding out another person's readiness to join some group political action. The social paradigm tells us there are ways to go about these interactions and ways not to do so. Indeed, from within a social paradigm, there are behaviors that would never occur to a person who is thoroughly of that society.

In 14th century Western Europe, the social paradigm was in flux. Massive change was mounting to a point that rendered tomorrow so much harder to guess, it no doubt generated a miasma of anxiety, felt with special intensity by the left-behinds mired in old systems that no longer applied or were becoming obsolete. One social paradigm had stopped working, a new one was emerging, and in this context, much that was happening looked meaningless.

This, I contend, is the most important ingredient of historical settings that provide lush soil for Truther Narratives to germinate and sprout. I'm suggesting that Truther Narratives prosper when pervasive social change is making the world so widely unrecognizable that a paradigm shift is in the works. The archetypal Truther Narrative is perfectly honed to making inexplicable events meaningful by placing them in an overall picture that is easy to grasp and in which all the parts fit with all the parts.

After the Paradigm Shift

In 1350, Western Europe was in transition from "the medieval period" to … something else. By 1450, however, most historians would agree that the transition was a fait accompli. The Black Death had waned; the Crusades were receding from memory; the feudal order was fading. Castles were relics on their way to becoming tourist attractions. Commerce was humming busily through networks of roads and sea lanes connecting towns and cities. The medieval period was over: Europe had entered a new era.

At the time, people probably simply thought of it as "nowadays" as opposed to "olden times". Historians retrospectively call it by names such as "the Renaissance" and later "the Enlightenment". Whatever the preferred name might be, a new social paradigm had settled into place in Europe; and sure enough, Truther Narratives seemed to recede to the margins of society for a few centuries.

This doesn't mean life was peaceful now and everyone was friends. Social paradigm doesn't mean social harmony. People were arguing as heatedly as ever; but they knew what they were arguing about. They didn't have the same answers, but they had the same questions. They didn't agree, but they shared terms of discourse. People were still fighting but they knew what they were fighting about; or against; or over, or for. The wars of religion early in this period were especially savage, but the contending sides all knew what the stakes were, which leads me to suggest: it isn't violence that stokes the Truther Narrative, it's meaningless violence; or perhaps, more precisely—meaninglessness itself.

The new paradigm still had issues to resolve and kinks to work out, but that's how it is with paradigmatic social orders. Once they're in place, they give the world a feeling of permanence. In actuality, of course, every social order is always in the process of changing in a myriad small ways, no matter how stable it might seem. A social paradigm takes whatever shape works best for the context that exists. The context being always in flux, the paradigm has to adjust constantly to stay functional. There's always some grinding of gears as these adjustments take place, but in "normal times" the gear-grinding is mostly minor. The world that people fall asleep in each night is pretty much the world they wake up in the next morning.

In the post-medieval period, one epic drama playing out on the European stage was the contest between Faith and Reason. Many people probably experienced this drama as issues they were grappling with in their own particular life stories. That is after all what history is mainly made of: lots of individual people grappling with the particular dramas of their own life stories. But all the small lives intertwining become visible as history when you move back far enough to see the larger patterns. And the drama we're titling Faith versus Reason reflected an epic story unfolding at this time: European Christianity was fragmenting into a Catholic

Church and many Protestant churches, plus a smattering of folks who belonged to no church at all.

At first, virtually everyone considered themselves affiliated with Faith. The question was only, Which faith? Which fragment of Christianity to embrace?

Then a smattering of folk started shifting their reliance from Faith to something they called Reason, and they began posing questions Faith had trouble answering. By the 17th century, more and more people were asking those difficult questions. Galileo might have been the most famous example, but he was only the tip of the iceberg. He died in 1642, and Isaac Newton was born 1643—the very next year: in short, the movement of thought was continuous.

On the continent philosophers such as Descartes and Leibniz were constructing a world-view built as purely as they could manage on scientific and mathematical principles alone. Many were starting to regard Reason as the protagonist of a heroic epic now in progress, and if reason was the protagonist, Faith by implication was the antagonist—unless one lined up with Faith, of course, in which case, Reason was the antagonist. Faith and Reason were playing different roles, but they were in the same drama, on the same stage. Both sides knew what their struggle was about: the authority to declare what was true. All this had nothing to do with the Truther Narrative: there was nothing marginal about this struggle: it was, in fact, one of the major mainstream stories of the age.

This mainstream story was reflected, however, in Truther Narrative, which had gone quiescent but never extinct. In Spain, anti-Semitism had intensified in virulence. The anti-Semitic Truther Narrative didn't go through any major permutations. It still centered on the Jews, a conspicuous and powerless minority, but the Inquisition, which was burning Jews to death as heretics in this period, did add one note. It declared Jewishness something a person could not renounce or abandon because Jewishness, it declared, wasn't a belief or an opinion but an inborn trait. This idea was already implicit in the anti-Semitism descended from medieval times, but the Inquisition made it explicit. Science didn't exist yet, but once science did exist, this tweak would become significant.

The other version of the Truther Narrative, the Secret Society version, which targeted a cosmopolitan elite, was the one to watch at this point. It lingered on as stories muttered among eccentrics in the cracks and crannies of society. It was easy to discount or ignore but there in the margins of society, the Secret Society template of Truther Narrative was quietly morphing and mutating. In retrospect, one can see how these mutations were responses to the mainstream story of the age, the contest between Faith and Reason.

Remember that, according to the secret-society version of the Truther Narrative, an unknown group with evil powers was among us, operating incognito to make bad things happen. People who circulated such stories no doubt added embellishments that felt like improvements to the flavor that made these stories appealing to the storytellers: the evil group became more evil and harder to spot. The evil ones didn't call themselves Templars anymore, they were going by a different name. They didn't dress in special outfits now, they looked like anyone. They were suspiciously insular however —they thought they were better than ordinary folks. This was a key point: they thought they were better. Any group closed to outsiders or secretive about its doings might be them, or at least might be agents of a hidden power secretly manipulating everyday life.

Rosicrucians

There were several groups on whom suspicion settled, in these early centuries of the post-feudal era. Among the earliest were the Rosicrucians, who weren't actually a group at all. At this point, the stories were barely discernible as Truther Narrative, if at all. In common usage the term Rosicrucian was more adjective than noun: it referred to an intellectual style or leaning, not unlike "beatnik" in the Fifties, or "countercultural" in the Sixties, or "progressive" these days.

People with "Rosicrucian" ideas believed in things like using education to improve the world. They took an interest in things like alchemy—which they were starting to call "chemistry." They tended to think the Pope had too much authority and to doubt that any king was entitled to absolute power. You might say "Rosicrucian" described the liberal intellectuals at the secular end of the Reason crowd.

Rosicrucians might have struck some people as insular because they preferred socializing among themselves to hanging out with the hoi polloi. That's not so strange if they were advanced intellectuals exploring the cutting edge ideas of their time. Princeton physics professors don't typically hang out at truck stops, looking for lively conversations about quantum mechanics with auto mechanics. But also, Rosicrucian ideas were still a little risky to trumpet at this point, for power still belonged to aristocrats, and monarchs were still absolute.

There were, however, people in European society who readily described themselves as Rosicrucian. Some of them also referred to themselves as natural philosophers. And some of these Rosicrucian natural philosophers did, actually, form a loose network, in that they were in correspondence with one another. They referred to themselves as …

Wait for it…

The Invisible College.

Whoa. If you were the type of person drawn to Truther Narrative, your ears might perk up at the sound of that.

And who was part of this Invisible College? Oh, people like Isaac Newton and Robert Boyle. They were the alchemists of their age, dabbling in magic, but it was a new kind of magic, the kind that came to be known as Science. In 1660, they established a formal society with a closed membership, yes a closed membership, which they called the

Royal Society. Here, members could huddle with one another and talk about their new type of magic. These were, in short, a 17th century European version of the college-educated intellectual elite, a demographic that in 21st Century America, Alt-Right Truther Narrative peddlers have fulminated about vociferously.

Sometime in the mid-1600s, Rosicrucian became a noun: there were murmurs about something called the "Rosicrucian Order". The term stemmed from three anonymous books circulating in Germany at that time. They purported to be centuries-old documents: they told of a man named Christian Rosenkreuz, who traveled through India and the Islamic World collecting esoteric knowledge, which enabled him to perform such feats as bringing the dead back to life.

According to these books, Rosenkreuz deemed his teachings too potent for the masses, so he founded a secret brotherhood and initiated nine men into it, each of whom was charged with passing the secret knowledge on to one successor before he died. So a secret order consisting of nine leaders had been operating incognito ever since.

The Rosicrucian Order was fiction, but in the 1600s, the core "texts" about the Rosicrucians were passed off as "rediscovered historical artifacts". In reality, of course, they were not rediscovered then but written then. Decades later, a theologian named Johann Valentin Andreae confessed to having written at least one of them as a joke.

But if you had the sort of itch that Truther Narrative is so good at scratching, you might have believed everything you heard about the Rosicrucians except that they were good—for if doing good was their mission and they had supernatural powers, why did bad things still happen? If you believed that a Rosicrucian Order really existed and you looked for concrete information about it, you might find it very suspicious that no one knew where their headquarters were or who their leaders were. If you were already suspicions about Rosicrucians, you might point to their logo—yes they had a logo; it came from the books: a cross with a rose at the center, hence the name Rosicrucian.

A red cross? Holy cow! A red cross was the very emblem the Templars carried on their shields! With this connection in place, Rosicrucian stories could tap the Templar archives for a wealth of details that fit right in. If you were the type to see a pattern where none existed, you might discern a plot…

In the 17th century, suspicions of this sort remained the harmless fantasies of fringe folks, no doubt recounted with many a chuckle at elegant parties where sophisticated intellectuals drank fine wines and discussed the secular ideas that would dominate the age to come. The context did not yet exist for Truther Narrative to flourish.

Masons

Then in 1717, a group of men given to Rosicrucian ideas and calling themselves Speculative Freemasons met in a

London tavern and organized a "lodge", a special type of members-only club. In their first meeting, these men elected one of themselves as "Grand Master." A strangely theatrical title, wouldn't you say? Then a similar group formed in Scotland, then one in France; and then Masonic lodges started popping up all across the continent. How suspicious was that? They all came with rules of membership, secret handshakes, and special rituals by which members might know each other in public without betraying any of their secrets.

The original Freemasons were a guild of medieval stone cutters involved in building cathedrals. They had initiation rites and insisted that anyone who wanted to be a Freemason had to learn a body of sacred knowledge, which only the guild could impart. The guild was merely doing what guilds do: preserving the value of its craft by controlling who became a mason and how many masons there could be. Professional associations do something similar today by licensing and limiting the practitioners of, say, medicine, or law.

When Masonic Lodges started forming in the 18th century, they didn't cut stone, but they did adopt the forms and structures of the original Masonic Lodges, with initiation rites for new members. To join a lodge, a man had to be sponsored by someone who was already a member. Masons had secret signals by which members could recognize one another in public, and teachings they did not share with outsiders. They had procedures by which members could rise to higher degrees as they mastered more of the teachings. To me, these practices foreshadow the structure of social status and advancement in the academic world of modern times. But to the suspicious-minded of the time, they echoed in ghostly fashion the stories told about the Assassins of Syria and Persia, the quasi-Islamic cult the Templars were accused of having joined when the kings and popes of Europe put them on trial for heresy.

When I was reading up on the Free Masons of the 18th century, their secretive rituals reminded me of the shenanigans boys get up to when they form "clubs". I was a boy once, so I know something about these shenanigans: what's the point of a club if membership isn't a privilege hard to obtain ?

What also struck me, however, was the social function the Masonic lodges must have provided and to whom they provided it. People developing an affinity for secular ideas were separating themselves from Church. But any given Church isn't just a complex of beliefs and rituals; it's also a social network. People go to church to gab with neighbors, share stories, share meals, join projects of mutual benefit...

If you're separating from the church into which you were born, you're also separating yourself from a world of social ties. How do you replace the ties you're giving up? In the 18th century, it appears, one thing you could do was join a Masonic lodge, if they'd let you in. It struck me that Masonry was like church for nascent secular humanists.

Faith still had a lot of clout, though. Most Europeans still went to regular churches, Catholic or Protestant. The Church as an institution still shaped public disapproval and it frowned on intellectual ideas and attitudes that eroded the credibility and prestige of Church as an institution in society per se.

This is just what the Reason crowd was getting up to by the 18th century, especially the extremists at the secular end. Masonic lodges were basically hi-faluting discussion clubs for people who wanted to bat around ideas they wouldn't feel comfortable sharing with the uneducated masses. People didn't face physical punishment for voicing Masonic ideas, but social shaming inflicts a punishment of its own. It makes sense to me therefore that Masons might be somewhat insular.

For the same reason, however, in the decades leading up to the French Revolution, the Freemasons' insularity and elitism made them the targets of Truther Narratives bubbling up. But the context still wasn't quite ripe for such stories to go viral. There were lots of arguments going on in European society, and the din was rising, but it hadn't reached the point of producing a top-to-bottom transformation of the European social world—not yet.

Illuminati

Then came the Illuminati, a club that lasted about two years before it got clubbed by a local duke, Karl-Theodore of Bavaria. The Illuminati was founded in 1776 by a certain Johann Adam Weishaupt, a professor of something or other at the University of Ingolstadt. Weishaupt had been a Jesuit once but quit. He had dabbled in Masonry once but quit. The Masons wanted to improve the world in the long run. The long run was way too long for Weishaupt. He wanted to save the world right now, with the truth-finding tools that secular wisdom offered: he wanted to educate the people, seek democracy, bring down the pope, and promote equality among all people. You might say he was radically Rosicrucian.

Weishaupt's club appealed to German intellectuals because it reflected the ferment of the times. A bunch of Illuminati clubs sprang up across Bavaria, complete with initiation rites and formal rules aping the pattern of Masonic lodges. It was Masonry for the emerging middle classes. Within two years, some 3,000 people across Bavaria called themselves Illuminati. The exact number is hard to specify since the Illuminati never actually existed as an organization. They were separate clubs that shared nothing except a sensibility, an attitude. If nothing had happened to them, they would have unraveled on their own and vanished from historical memory.

But something did happen to them: Karl-Theodore happened to them. He saw people huddling in cafes, muttering about one-world government, and he saw trouble for dukes. Weishaupt had written that only the well-educated should rule and Duke Karl knew what *that* meant. The

Church agreed with him: the Illuminati were out to abolish religion and promote atheism. For the good of society, they had to be stopped. So the duke outlawed the Illuminati, shut down their clubs, banished Weishaupt, and drove all the Illuminati types he could find into exile.

By eliminating them from Bavaria, the Duke made them realer than they ever were. He gave them an aura of menace they never actually had. The Duke gave Truther Narrative something to build a story around. Once the actual Illuminati were gone, the Illuminati could become whatever the story needed them to be. It was the same dynamic that animated the Templar myth, and the Jewish moneylender myth. Each Conspiracy Theorist whispering about the Illuminati "improved" the narrative with details that intensified the shivers Truther Narrative delivers to its believers.

According to the narrative emerging now, the Illuminati were a tightly organized politically-motivated unit organized for one frightening goal: total world domination. When the Illuminati said One World Government, *that's* what they meant. If you couldn't spot any real-life Illuminati on the streets, it only proved how good they were at staying hidden—because they were around all right: oh, they were everywhere. But the Illuminati were organized in ranks that formed a pyramid; only a tiny ring of people at the very top knew what was really going on. This was exactly the same mode of organization attributed to the Assassins of Syria, who came to Christendom disguised as Templars. In fact, some said the Illuminati *were* the Templars.

Long 19th Century:
The French Revolution and Its Aftermath

With the Illuminati, we come to the brink of the next historical setting that stands out as a particularly fertile one for the Truther Narrative: I'm talking about Europe and its environs in the aftermath of the French Revolution. The generation that was coming of age when the Illuminati was founded was the generation that went through the French Revolution in their forties and fifties. Their world view was formed in the decades leading up to that Revolution.

In those decades, the world was getting messy and incoherent at a dizzying pace. In France, the countryside was full of angry peasants with nothing to lose. Across continental Europe, towns were full of people who wanted to throw a brick every time they saw a duke. In Paris, wage slaves were living in slums while clergy lolled in luxury, and aristocrats idled their days away playing trivial games in fancy mansions.

This was also a time when more people were learning how to read, just as more and more books were being published about how everyone was equal, and how reason was more important than faith. Among the moderately well-off, so-called literary societies a.k.a. reading clubs a.k.a. discussion clubs were sprouting in many cities, towns, and villages: these were largely clubs for people who wanted to discuss (and fulminate about) the growing incoherence of society. Stir those ingredients well, and you can see a revolution coming.

Not only was social change accelerating but money was moving abruptly to a higher level of abstraction. By this time, ordinary folks in Europe had absorbed the earlier tide of abstractions such as paper money, and bills of exchange that were buyable and sellable as if they were actual goods on a par with barrels of hog-lard. Paper instruments like these had acquired a feel of tangible value almost on a par with coins.

But disturbing new forms of money were rising out of the soil of the economy, leading to inexplicable phenomena such as "financial bubbles". A striking early example was the Tulip Frenzy of 1636. That year, the price of tulips suddenly began to rise in northwestern Europe. It rose so dramatically, people were paying the price of a house for a tulip. Any sensible person would have said, for God's sake, what are you thinking? Then—the price of tulips crashed, as if everyone had woken up from a dream. How could anyone not have seen that coming? Well, lots of people didn't. They jumped in feet first and ended up on their butts, begging for spare change.

The Tulip Frenzy presaged stock bubbles. How stocks could work as stored money required some puzzling out on the part of common folk. Stocks were supposedly "shares" of some enterprise happening so far away you couldn't see it. Most people who owned shares had nothing to do with said enterprise, had never witnessed any of it with their own eyes, had no dead-bang proof the enterprise even really existed. In 1720, there was an enterprise of this kind in Britain, called the South Sea Company, whose shares were soaring in value for a while. Then one day they simply crashed. Most people couldn't fathom why they had soared or why they had crashed.

The same thing happened in France with the so-called Mississippi Bubble. This one nearly brought down the whole financial system of France. It happened because a Scotsman named John Law—briefly the finance minister of France—had a scheme. His scheme had something to do with basing the currency of the country on stock that could work like money, in that you could buy big-ticket items like land with it, but there was nothing tangible backing it, no gold, no silver, nothing. What backed it was only the story of some project on the Mississippi River in North America that few had seen in person. Law wanted to float the country's currency as a capital derivative at a fixed interest rate of cumulatively indexed values that—okay, I apologize: I'll stop. I'll stop. I'm just making up all those terms. I don't understand what John Law was doing or why he thought it would work, or why it didn't, or why it should have. Money at this level of abstraction doesn't make sense to me, and I'm looking at it with 21st century eyes. I can't imagine what the ordinary 18th century French person could have made of what John Law, the finance minister of their country, was doing to make their country's paper currency work as money. I only know that lots of people thought they understood enough about his new form of money to lose their shirts (as many people have done in recent times with cryptocurrency).

I also know, because I'm living so much later, that Law actually had a viable idea. He just couldn't figure out quite how to make it work. Since then, I'm told, other countries have tried versions of his ideas (whatever they were) and succeeded. Apparently, Law wasn't a crook, he was just a man ahead of his time, a man dealing with money at a level of abstraction his society could not fathom. In 18th century France, the man-on-the-street could only scratch his head. And if he was one of the many ruined by the Mississippi Bubble, he might do more than scratch his head. He might go out and break something.

World History—the Truthers' Version

Conventional history tells us that the French Revolution erupted in 1789 when a mob of ordinary folks stormed a big prison in Paris and released the prisoners. Discussion clubs immediately seized a central role in the upheaval that soon began to swell. Most important were the Jacobins, very popular with the emerging middle classes. Their leaders were mostly lawyers, clerks, doctors, journalists, and the like. Analogous figures today might be folks working for startups, providing IT to companies, inventing apps. Many of the most famous names associated with the revolution—Danton, Robespierre, St. Juste, Desmoulins, Marat—belonged to Jacobin Clubs. In 1790, there were about 120 of these clubs. By 1792, their number had ballooned to 7,000 and the membership to half a million or more. The Jacobins were the most powerful of the discussion clubs but not the only one. The Girondists were another, the Sans-Culotte another; and there were other smaller, lesser-known networks. The Revolution raged for ten or twelve years and then the dust began to settle, and Europe returned to normal.

Except, it wasn't the old normal. If one could have compared snapshots of the western European social cosmos 50 years before the French Revolution and 50 years after, they'd look like two entirely different worlds. The events that began with the storming of the Bastille triggered a paradigm shift, not just in France, but across Europe as a whole. In the tensions building up to the revolution, and then in the aftermath of that Revolution, two unrelated social paradigms were in play: the old one that was growing obsolete and a new one that was still taking shape. Some people were making meaning with the old reference points, some with the new. The resulting incoherence gave Truther Narrative the context it needed to gnaw its way out of the corners and lay claim to being the one explanation that could make sense of this crazy world.

In the next period, the long 19th century as it is sometimes called, the secret society template of Truther Narrative went through significant mutations. One of these was the emergence of a Truther Narrative of history itself. I used to think no one would try to explain broad historical developments such as the collapse of the Roman Empire, or the Reformation, or the French Revolution as products of conspiracies by small, secret groups, but I was wrong. I discovered this one day when, just for laughs, I googled French Revolution and Conspiracy Theory and, to my surprise, got hundreds of hits. The French Revolution, it turns out, was a prime obsession of Conspiracy Theorists in the long 19th century and beyond. In the immediate aftermath of the revolution, Truther Narrative found professorial practitioners who used the secret society template to develop something like a pseudo-academic theory of history—a mutant theory, I would call it, clad in professorial pomp, but a theory of history nonetheless. It was Truther Narrative scaled up to global dimensions.

A raft of books and articles published after the revolution laid the groundwork for this Conspiracy-Theory of History. They were books like *Memoirs Illustrating the History of Jacobinism* by French cleric Abbe Augustin Barruel; and *Proofs of a Conspiracy: Against All The Religions and Governments Of Europe, Carried On In The Secret Meetings of Freemasons, Illuminati, and Reading Societies,* by John Robison, a professor of natural history at the University of Edinburgh.

These writers (among others) declared the French Revolution to have been the product of a plot by a small group of men—an evil cabal. Robison "proved" that this cabal was descended directly from the Knights Templar through the Masons by tracing the connections back through the centuries link by link, with footnotes set forth in correct academic fashion. He wrote that this cabal was a triple alliance between the Freemasons, the Illuminati, and the "Sophisters"—a sinister, well-organized gang of so-called philosophers with a history of undermining morality and corrupting youth. They included people like Voltaire, Diderot, Montesquieu, and Rousseau. The Triple Conspiracy had crafted clever appeals to "toleration", "reason", and "humanity", said Barruel, in order to mesmerize simpletons who imagined themselves to be oppressed. The Cabal, he wrote, had cleverly filled the minds of the masses with words like Liberty and Equality—to pave the way for violence and murder.

According to these new Conspiracy Theorists, the storming of the Bastille was not a spontaneous event carried out by a mob of desperate Parisians. It was enacted by well-paid actors carrying out orders from above. The people fielding this preposterous narrative started a line of Truther Narrative that runs right to the present day: consider the Sandy Hook Deniers, who claimed that the hideous massacre of children at an elementary school in Connecticut in 2012 didn't actually happen at all: according to these deniers, it was all staged—children, shooters, and parents, all were actors. The 19th century Conspiracy Theorists "explaining" the French Revolution pioneered this idea that selected news events might actually be scripted dramas.

These Conspiracy Theorists provided the date on which the French Revolution plot was finalized and set in motion. It happened one night, they said, in 1786, at a secret meeting in Frankfurt-am-Main, attended by a small ring of men led by a fellow named Louis Philippe II, the fifth Duke of Orleans. Who was this man, really? Well, you can look him up. He was in his day one of the richest men in France and a patron of France's emerging liberal intelligentsia. He found the works of Jean-Jacques Rousseau inspiring. He dropped in on meetings of the Jacobin Clubs. He was against feudalism and slavery. You might say his ideas were downright Rosicrucian. The Conspiracy Theorists said the French Revolution was his evil scheme.

Their suspicions fell on this man in particular because he had been Grand Master of a prominent Masonic lodge. He'd distanced himself from Freemasonry since those days, but he couldn't fool the professors of Conspiracy Theory. They recognized all the signs of a secret society covering its tracks. These 19th century Conspiracy Theorists noted that the Duc d'Orléans had the cash to buy "idea men". Academic historians identify Mirabeau as a towering player in the first days of the revolution: Conspiracy Theorists saw him as a bought-and-paid-for stooge, carrying out orders from above. Historians see men like Abbe Sieyès, Camille Desmoulins, Danton, Robespierre, and Marat as flamethrowing radical revolutionaries. The Conspiracy Theorists of post-Revolution France saw them as mindless minions of the Duc d'Orléans, actors reading lines scripted for them by the cabal's propagandists.

At that meeting in Frankfürt, the Conspiracy Theorists wrote, the cabal decided that bringing all of humanity under its grip would require destroying the church, erasing monarchy as an institution, and putting an end to all civil order. They schemed out how this could be done and decided it would require replacing sacred values with debased alternatives that bred isolation and despair. Once the people had been sufficiently dislocated and confused, the cabal would finalize its dream of enslaving all of humanity. Toward this end, they mapped out a multi-year plan, designed to put the king and queen of France to death on a certain date. Sure enough, on that date in 1792, right on schedule, they were able to march Louis XVI and Marie Antoinette right to the guillotine.

Two Prototypes Merge

The two prototype Truther Narratives that germinated in the 14th Century had much in common, but they also had one notable difference. The anti-Semitic Truther Narrative featured a recognizable Other. *Recognizable* was the essential point. You knew who the Jews were. Even if you had never seen one, you believed you knew what to look for. After all, what was the use of having someone to hate and fear and blame if you couldn't even picture who that someone was?

The other version of Truther Narrative featured a group of people one could *not* recognize. Templars masqueraded as ordinary folks. In this version, *unrecognizable* was the most essential point: they looked like us, pretended to *be* one-of-us, but were actually *them*. A core feature of this Secret Society version of Truther Narrative was its proposition that the enemy is already inside.

About midway through the century that followed the French Revolution, these two templates merged to form a single new Truther Narrative, in which all the elements of the anti-Semitic Truther Narrative were poured into the Secret Society template. An artifact called *The Protocols of the Elders of Zion* played a crucial role in producing this new, hybrid theory. The document has a complex history, but if you follow it chronologically you can see how it ended up pumping fuel into the horrors perpetrated by Nazi Germany.

The story begins with Napoleon Bonaparte's nephew Louis Napoleon. In 1848, this blowhard got himself elected president of the French Republic. A few years later, he shut down democracy and declared himself absolute emperor. People who embraced liberal ideals such as elections, free speech, and separation of church and state protested, but Emperor Napoleon shut them up by putting them in prison.

A lawyer named Maurice Joly wrote a searingly critical satire of the emperor, but without naming Napoleon. He wrote it as a Platonic dialog between two thinkers who take turns making the case for two opposing political positions. He called it *Dialogue in Hell Between Machiavelli and Montesquieu.* The real Montesquieu was a liberal Enlightenment thinker. The real Machiavelli was the Renaissance-era author of *The Prince,* a handbook of cynical advice for rulers.

Joly gave Montesquieu all the good-guy lines: arguments for fairness, decency, and democracy. He gave Machiavelli all the lines an evil, ruthless, manipulative, power-hungry son-of-a-bitch bastard would say, including boastful declarations about subverting the popular will and getting the people to hunger for tyranny. Joly published his book anonymously, but the emperor's men found him out and put him in prison, where he committed suicide. His book was banned and forgotten; but a few copies survived.

And now: let's follow a completely separate stream of events. In 1868, a rabidly anti-Semitic trash-novelist named Hermann Goedsche wrote a lurid thriller called *Biarritz*. In one chapter titled *At the Jewish Cemetery in Prague*, twelve sinister supernatural figures issue from tombs for a meeting under cover of night. They are "the Elders of Zion", leaders of the twelve Jewish tribes of yore, inhuman monsters who have been scheming for centuries to gain control of the world: they rise from their graves every hundred years to discuss how their schemes are going. *Biarritz* failed to find an audience and lapsed into obscurity, but a few copies survived in musty second-hand bookstores.

And now the plot thickens.

In the early 1900s, Czarist Russia was in a state of revolutionary ferment. Anti-Semitism had long been a toxic presence in Russian culture, and it was raging now, among Czarist right-wingers. One such group was the Black Hundred, whose slogan was "Save Russia! Kill the Jews!" They had a newspaper of their own called *Znamya*. In 1903, the Black Hundred published a "shocking" document "recently discovered." It was an 80-page pamphlet which the editors said they had received from a "reliable source". They didn't mention that the source was the Okhrana, the Czar's secret police. *Znamya* titled the pamphlet *The Protocols of the Elders of Zion* and said it was the verbatim transcript of an actual secret meeting held by the Elders of Zion, a committee made up of twelve Jewish princes bent on reducing humanity to slavery.

The Okhrana had, of course, created the document, not "discovered" it. But they hadn't bothered to actually write something. They'd cobbled the pamphlet together from pre-existing bits. They'd lifted the plot wholesale from the novel *Biarritz*. They'd plagiarized the minutes of the meeting verbatim from Joly's *Dialog in Hell*, leaving out all the lines spoken by Joly's Montesquieu character and including only the lines spoken by the Machiavelli character. The Okhrana presented these lines as the actual words spoken by an actual cabal of twelve evil Jews.

The Okhrana produced the pamphlet as red meat for the Czar's "base", and it worked. Readers of *Znamya* took the pamphlet exactly as the Okhrana had intended: as a historical artifact and as "evidence". Two years later, a Russian religious fanatic named Sergei Nilus included it as an appendix to his book *The Great in the Small: The Coming of the Anti-Christ and the Rule of Satan on Earth*. Nilus had a following, so his book took off, and by 1917 he had published four editions of the *Protocols* as a stand-alone booklet. Once it was out there, the *Protocols* spread like a weed, because the larger social and historical context favored it: the Western world had become ready compost for Truther Narrative. By 1920, translations of the *Protocols* had appeared in Poland, France, England, and elsewhere. Copies were traveling to Palestine, where European Jews inspired by Zionism were arriving in great numbers as migrants. There it fanned the flames between the Jews from Europe and the Arabs already inhabiting this land as their home.

The *Protocols* also made its way to the United States. Henry Ford, founder of the Ford Motor Company, read the *Protocols* and was so impressed, he had it published as a series in a newspaper he owned, the *Dearborn Independent*. The series was called *The International Jew: The World Problem Today*. It used the *Protocols* to build a case that Jews and Bolsheviks, working through Masonic lodges, were trying to weaken American culture as a prelude to conquering America. These Elders of Zion had secretly gained control of the American press except for a few daring outliers such as Ford's own *Dearborn Independent*. They were manipulating the economy through banking monopolies, using intellectuals to confuse real Americans, corrupting elected officials, and promoting jazz. Ford had 500,000 copies of *The International Jew* published and distributed. It was then translated into sixteen languages, including German. A lawsuit later forced him to retract the publication and issue an apology, which included his claim that he'd been duped. But he made no secret of his admiration for a man in Germany who embraced the Protocols without apology: Adolf Hitler.

Hitler quoted from *The Protocols of the Elders of Zion* in his tract *Mein Kampf*. He and Goebbels knew the *Protocols* was a crude fiction forged by the Russian secret police, and they actually admitted this openly, but they said it expressed the "inner truth". What Hitler and his cronies did see most definitely when they looked at the *Protocols* was a weapon. Anti-Semitism was rampant among the German working class, and they knew it. Truther Narrative tropes about a secret society bent on world conquest were rampant in popular culture and they knew it. The *Protocols of the Elders of Zion* melded these two templates into one: it said yes, there was a secret cabal: it was the Elders of Zion.

From the start, Truther Narrative had resonated among the struggling masses. When food was sparse, when the future was frightening, when no one knew what was true or even how to determine what was true, when people were angry, Truther Narrative gave them someone to be angry at. From the start, Truther Narrative also gave Lords with Swords an instrument with which to redirect the grievances of the exploited, away from themselves and toward some scapegoat vulnerable to the wrath of the masses. Hitler honed Truther Narrative into a fearful instance of such an instrument.

Whether he actually believed in a secret Jewish cabal of all-powerful bankers is not certain, but what he believed doesn't matter. What matters is the use he made of Truther Narrative. He and his cronies used it to help them manipulate the German electorate and seize control of the Weimar Republic. Then they launched a war that claimed 60 million lives and carried out the Holocaust in which six to ten million people were gassed or burned to death. They could not have done it without Truther Narrative.

How History (Actually) Happens

The story of the French Revolution told by 19th century Conspiracy Theorists was a stark drama featuring heroes and villains. A close look at that story exposes, I think, some of the key fallacies that make Truther Narrative inherently false. As an explanation of current events and of history in general, Truther Narrative is based on the idea that when life is "normal" nothing changes. It presumes that the baseline condition of human society is stasis. New things happen, sure; they happen every day, but the stage on which they happen is always the same: life is predictable. You just have to know the rules and follow them.

When the world becomes unpredictable—when the stage itself shifts, when the whole framework of reality turns dubious—it's someone's fault. When the stage itself starts changing, it's because some villain is messing with the stage. The Truthers' narrative of history sees vast world-changing historical events—eruptions of revolutionary fervor, the rise and fall of belief systems, the flux of empires—as plots by small secret groups. It identifies what action people should take in the face of accelerating change and mounting trouble: they should find and stop the hidden villains causing all this change: find them and stop them by whatever means necessary.

Most if not all academic historians would agree, I think, that the Truther Narrative version of history is wrong because it is based on one crucial false assumption—that stasis is the normal condition of social reality. In fact, change is the normal condition of the stage on which the human story unfolds. Like it or not, *that's* the reality. In small ways, change is happening all the time. In small ways it's happening everywhere. It can be shaped to some extent but it can't be halted or reversed. Last year's fashions aren't this year's fashions. This year's slang isn't next year's slang. Everyone used to wear hats in public, now most people don't. All cars used to run on gas, now some run on electricity. One neighborhood is getting gentrified, another is going downhill. Yesterday, Grandpa was alive, now he's dead. The neighbors never had a cat, now they do. Cousin Vicki never had children; now she's pregnant. That's the story of everyday life: constant change.

Tipping Points

Most changes are small, but small changes accumulate. Social changes accumulate until they strain the conventions that contain them. Structures that emerged in one historical context get out of synch with the way things are today. Problems come up that have no solutions within existing frameworks. Institutions that were developed to fix things, weren't made to fix *these* things, the things happening *now*.

Since social reality is always changing, the social system keeps getting out of synch with the actual social environment. Pressure starts to build, the way pressure does along a fault-line in the Earth where two tectonic plates are pressed together and pushing in opposite directions. In geology, when a slippage finally occurs, it's called an earthquake. In history, when change finally accumulates to a breaking point, something like the French Revolution happens.

A historian looking at the French Revolution would observe that French society's various parts had been slowly getting out of synch for decades, even centuries. This was true of Europe in general, but it was more powerfully so in the case of France. For example, the mechanisms of the French government were based on the assumption that there were three distinct classes of people in society, three "estates" as the French called them: landowning aristocrats, clerics, and peasants. Topping the whole pyramid was the king.

By the 18th century, however, the three Estates didn't really describe French society at all. An ever-growing number of people belonged to none of those three estates. Many belonged to a new and ever-growing class of folks that was coming into existence because of the rise of cities, the rise of commerce, and the ever-growing importance of manufacturing. They included an ever-burgeoning cadre of information-management workers such as lawyers and bookkeepers and other experts generated by the growing complexity of French society: the proliferation of its moving parts.

All these managers, merchants, sales professionals, lawyers and whatnot had real power because they were crucial to the economy and to keeping the currents of everyday life flowing; but politically they had no power. The mechanisms of government had formed when society was different. There were no mechanisms that took all these new types of people into account. Of course there was going to be a revolution, just as the seams of a suit of clothes made for a toddler burst if he/she keeps wearing them into adulthood. Lots of people contributed to the revolution, but no single anyone or anything *caused* it. In all likelihood no one could have prevented *something* like the French Revolution from happening. A time had come when France just had to shrug off its old political and social apparatus and reconfigure itself to become what it was now.

Once it had institutions that fit the new reality, a new world came into being. Even as it did, however, that world was on its way to becoming outdated, because reality kept doing what reality keeps doing; it kept changing, and changes accumulate. A similar thing is underway today when, for example, the economy is becoming a global phenomenon while the political and social instruments for managing that economy are still largely national.

Ripple Effects

Another unavoidable factor in real history is the ripple effects phenomenon. No human or group of humans lives all alone, isolated from the rest of humanity. Even a remote tribe in the heart of the Amazon jungle or the highest habitable slopes of the Andes or the furthest northern regions of Siberia knows of other tribes and has at least occasional interactions with them. Whatever humans do affects what other nearby humans do; and their reactions affect humans further afield. And since everyone is connected to everyone, whatever goes around comes around. In no social location can people fully know what ripple effects they're sending out or which ones will be coming back. No one can know where the incoming ripple effects originated and where new ones are coming from now.

With big events such as the French Revolution, one can see in retrospect many different ripple effects flowing from many different locations, into and through the Revolution. All were causes, all were effects, and none was definitive. History is a fabric woven of ripple effects. And if you're looking for somewhere solid to stand, good luck; because everything in social reality is made of ripples.

Chaos Theory

Add ripple effects to the picture and what you have is staggering complexity. Complexity means that historical explanations are limited by chaos theory. James Gleick set forth this theory as a mathematical concept in his book *Chaos: The Making of a New Science*. As I understand it, Gleick is saying that when one looks at cause-and-effect in the physical universe, one can use the laws of physics to calculate what's going to happen—but only up to a point. If two billiard balls are rolling toward each other, one can predict, at least in theory, which way they'll roll and how far they'll go after they collide. One can make this prediction based on objective data including the shape, weight, direction, and speed of each ball. It's just numbers.

But:

If there are three balls on the table, things get exponentially more complicated. You'll need more data. It will have to be more precise. And if you keep adding balls, there comes a point past which the effects of any cause cannot be calculated from information about the original conditions. It's not just a physical impossibility, it's a theoretical impossibility, a mathematical impossibility. If a butterfly flaps its wings in Japan, a chain of causal links might be found to a storm in Texas. Some people interpret chaos theory to mean, a butterfly flapping its wings can cause a hurricane. That, I think, is a misreading. Chaos Theory is saying that causal explanations have a limit to their explanatory power. Chaos Theory describes a profound metaphorical truth about real history. Ultimately, we humans are surrounded, not just by the unknown but by … the unknowable.

This being the case, no tightly organized little group of humans can *plan* to cause a sweeping historical event and actually bring it about. They can try, of course, and people do try: they hatch plots, they take steps…but what they can't do is dictate what their steps will lead to. Ultimately, what ends up happening won't be what they planned because they can't insulate themselves from the ripple effects coming back at 'em.

The fundamental flaw in the Truther Narrative explanation of history isn't that some small group can't *trigger* an enormous event. Small groups can and do. In 44 BC, a small group of senators in Rome plotted to kill Julius Caesar, the most powerful man in the world known to Romans. They succeeded—with momentous results.

Succeeded, yes, and momentous yes, but here's the hitch. The momentous results weren't what the plotters had envisioned. The men who murdered Caesar did so to "save the Republic"— the Rome into which they were born. They believed Caesar was trying to bring back monarchy, trying to make himself king. They believed they could stem that tide by killing him.

What they did, however, by assassinating Caesar, was to trigger a civil war that ended with Caesar's adopted son Octavian overcoming all his rivals and establishing himself as the absolute ruler of Rome and all its lands. The men who killed Caesar to save the republic set in motion the events that put an end to the Republic and turned Rome into an empire ruled by a single man with unlimited powers. That's irony, but it's also just plain old history. Plots happen but plots that actually shape history to the needs and desires of the plotters? Not really ever, I'm betting.

Black Swans

There's one final factor not to be ignored, which Nassim Taleb set forth in his book *The Black Swan*. Taleb observed that on any given day, something might happen that could not have been predicted from the evidence available yesterday. That might seem like a truism, and yet—think about it. In everyday life, we base our plans and decisions on what we "know" to be possible or impossible, based on all our experiences so far, and we take those factors into account as we steer among the rocks of reality, trying to reach our goals. But we don't know everything. On any given day, new experiences might reveal that something we "know" to be true is actually false. To paraphrase Taleb, suppose we've based our plans on the knowledge that swans are white, which we know to be true because all the swans we've ever seen were white; and then one day we see a Black Swan. One black swan and suddenly the all-swans-are-white postulate crumbles out of existence and so does everything built on that postulate. We're left not knowing what color a swan might be—or any bird, really. Or anything, maybe.

The color of swans might not matter much to most, but metaphorically, Black Swans matter. Why? Because history is replete with them. The Covid pandemic was a Black Swan.

As far as I know, when 2019 began, no one was taking sudden-global-lockdown into account when crafting their life plans. Now, it's something we can't exclude from the list of things we maybe should be prepared for. What we can't add to that list is a thing that would never occur to us. We know those things exist. We can't know what they are. Therefore, people cannot control history. They can respond to history, they can affect history, but no one can control it.

Clues from History

If we think of Truther Narrative as a virus with a life of its own, it's possible to discern why it might be more active in some historical settings than in others. We can discern at least some of the pertinent elements these settings share. For one thing, these are periods and places when money is jumping to a higher level of abstraction. For another, these are epochs when social change is accumulating to a tipping point, epochs when old narratives are losing their power to explain what's happening, but new narratives haven't achieved real coherence yet. In sum, these are times when the social paradigm of some whole society has become obsolete and a paradigm shift is either happening or is about to happen.

It makes sense that a culture's immune system is weak when old narratives are losing their power. Familiar narratives provide ready-made stencils by which to make meaning of the things that happen each day. In normal times, most of what we encounter is more or less familiar, most of it fits into the big-picture we already have, so the familiar narratives are handy tools. When we see something, we more or less know what it is because we've seen something like it before. All we have to work out in each moment are the foreground elements, the things that stand out against the unchanging background: the things that matter right now.

When something unexpected happens in such a context, we can go on high alert to figure out what we're dealing with, and maybe we'll have to revise our big-picture a little as we're dealing with it, but then, when things return to normal we can settle back into the groove and keep a-going.

When old narratives are eroding, however, we can't relax. We have to stay mustered, because things won't go back to normal. Normal has gone out of existence. We don't know what's coming. We only know it'll be coming hard and fast. And we won't know what it is as it approaches, because the incoming dots of data won't readily form any single whole picture. So we'll have to ramp up that genetically embedded, connecting-the-dots mechanism we have as humans, and construct a new big-picture on the fly.

That means we'll have to be discerning patterns in a riot of data *quickly*. Our genes give us the need to see patterns, but the times? The times can make us *desperate* to see patterns, and that desperation is red meat for the virus that is the Truther Narrative. It can feed on that desperation by providing a simple basic template, into which all new data can be quickly fit or quickly discarded. And, as plenty of research has shown, those are circumstances in which we humans tend to spot hidden patterns that don't exist—one of the hallmarks of people infected with the Truther Narrative virus.

The Abstraction of Money

It also makes sense that a growing abstraction of money might provide opportunities for the Truther Narrative virus. Money, after all, is one of the most fundamental mechanisms of interconnectedness among us humans, and its workings depend on all of us sharing a sense of how all of us are measuring value.

It's one thing to discern how ones own self is measuring value. To ones own thoughts and feelings, one has direct access. It's another matter to discern how other people are measuring value. With no direct access to their thoughts and feelings, one has to go by what they say and by various external clues. But to sense how all-of-us are measuring value? That's another whole level of complexity altogether.

And in normal times, that's where culture comes in. Culture might be defined as that field of feelings and information to which all-of-us have more or less intuitive access—if we're part of the culture. If a culture loses coherence, "all-of-us" becomes chimerical, or difficult to discern; at the very least, we start to have trouble telling who is one-of-us and who isn't—or it comes to feel as if there is no such thing as all-of-us. In that case, the anxiety about hooking into the money system can't help but spike. It happens inevitably because we as individuals *must* hook into the money-system or we're dead, and this becomes disturbingly difficult when money becomes something we can't comprehend or even recognize. Any sudden change in the nature of money is therefore bound to compromise a culture's immune system, until people get used to it.

In the 14th century, when money suddenly jumped to a higher level of abstraction, the peasants were the left-behinds. In their world palpable use was the measure of value. It was crops and plows and horses and soil: things you could see and touch. Coins were a bit more abstract than crops and soil, but one could still see coins, touch coins, code them fairly unambiguously to "real" value. And, as mentioned, there was no mystery about why lords were at the top of the social pyramid. They owned the land and they had swords. It also made sense for clergy to possess a privileged position. They owned the narrative.

Today, older, wage-earning blue-collar industrial line workers might be compared to the peasant-farmers of medieval Europe. They were dealing with money at the most concrete level. Anyone could understand how to value an hourly wage (or a monthly salary). It was understandable why some work paid more than other work. It had to do with how hard the work was, what it contributed, how much training was required, how many people wanted the products of this work… This is not to say wage-earners or low-level salaried workers in a stable healthy society are happy with their wages. Anyone might feel that "it isn't fair, what they're paying me."

But the value created by a mineworker or a bus driver or a blue-collar line worker in a factory or a file clerk or a bookkeeper or a civil engineer can't be compared with the value created by a financial expert who is selling credit default derivatives and buying call-on-put futures options. Those are two different worlds of money, and let's face it: the latter is incalculably more abstract than the former. Against this background, it's not surprising that anxiety permeates the mood among wage-earning blue-collar workers and the rest of the jobs mentioned above at a time when all the jobs one can imagine having—all sources of the kind of money one understands—appear to be vanishing: because all work of the kind one knows how to do or might learn, are vanishing.

Anxiety of this type doesn't have to be about any particular thing. It's not like anxiety about the strange sound in one's car engine. A person can feel anxiety of this type without being able to pinpoint what they're worried about; they might be employed, and have no reason to fear they'll be fired or laid off in the next week or month, and yet feel anxious about their future prospects. And if you're anxious without knowing why, that's worrisome in itself. This kind of anxiety therefore feeds upon itself and grows. To a society in the throes of anxiety-syndrome, Truther Narrative has something seductive to offer: a concrete reason for the anxiety one feels and a concrete action one can take. Someone is *doing* this, the Truther Narrative whispers. Find that evil someone and stop him, her, or them. Kill if you must, it might eventually start muttering…

When the Social Paradigm Is Shifting

The erosion of old narratives and the growing abstraction of money are only subsets, however, of a larger phenomenon. It's when one social paradigm is giving way to another that Truther Narrative has a field day. A social paradigm, remember, is not this or that narrative. It's the relationship among all the narratives in operation. What makes the social paradigm functional is its overall coherence. All its parts more or less fit with all its parts. A different paradigm might have most of the same parts but the order among them will be different. They'll add up to a different picture, as it were. When the old paradigm was in place, everything made sense. When the new paradigm is in place, everything will make sense. But in the transition from one to the other, there is bound to be a time when the parts are many and the connections few.

Before paradigm shift | During paradigm shift | After paradigm shift

When a culture is going through a paradigm shift, it's teeming with disconnected fragments of ideas drifting about in the public conversation, available to bond with other fragments of ideas and become new narratives. In such an environment, Truther Narrative has the kind of muscle among competing narratives that gangs have in a social landscape when order breaks down. Truther Narrative can vacuum up idea-fragments faster than healthier narratives can compete with.

During a paradigm shift, the bases for being part of a group are changing. Shifting values turns people who used to be heroes into pariahs. It turns people who would have been losers into stars. Anxiety ramps up as people feel themselves falling out of sync with groups they recognize. And maybe in a larger sense, this is all just normal. Since a social paradigm exists only as the sum of the thoughts and feelings of all the individual people in a social galaxy, it can change only by virtue of a whole society's worth of individual people coming to see the world in a new way and in the *same* new way: it requires that a whole bunch of people change their collective mind.

There's no way this can happen quickly. Each person can only do what one person can do. How can that add up to a paradigm change? If a crowd could talk, that might be what the crowd is muttering as it finds its way from one global social paradigm to another. The emergence of numerous, tiny, tightly-knit niche groups might not mean the crowd isn't busy changing its mind. It might just mean the crowd is being cautious about which way it goes, because it doesn't want to risk getting separated from the rest of the crowd in the process of changing its collective mind. People feeling this threat will naturally melt in with whatever crowd is small enough to feel recognizable and real and able to hold on to a collective coherence. Inevitably, during such a transition, there will be a stage that is marked by the proliferation of what people have been calling social bubbles.

Part Three
Our World, Our Time

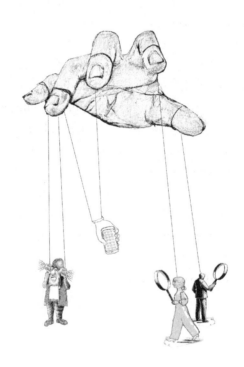

Why Now?

As we barrel through the 2020s, Truther Narrative seems to be flaring everywhere. Does this mean a global paradigm shift is about to happen? Or happening? It better be, because the old paradigm is so quickly growing obsolete.

The change we're in the middle of is, I submit, bigger and deeper than the ones associated with the World Wars of the 20th century, the French Revolution, or the transition from feudalism to post-feudalism. It's more like the transition from hunting and gathering to farming and herding—except, speeded up a thousand-fold. In America within the last century (and around the planet for that matter) social change has been undermining assumptions axiomatic for decades, for centuries, for millennia. In fact, some social changes now underway are bringing into question assumptions rooted in millions of years of human experience, going back to our days as pre-human bi-pedal primates.

Countries

Take, for example, verities embedded for mere decades that are already eroding and whose erosion is creating palpable disturbances, even though their roots be shallow. The nation-state is one prime example. Throughout my lifetime, people have understood the nation-state to be the fundamental political unit of humanity. Everyone has been navigating a planet divided into countries. Everyone has considered themselves to be living in one of these units. Their identity has deeply included what nation-state they're a member of. Each of these units have abutted on other such units with no space in between except in such places as Korea's DMZ. We 've been operating on the knowledge that every country has its own government, its own laws, its own currency. We know that every country has an official language, an army of its own, a police force of some kind, and a distinct identity expressed through such symbolic markers as a flag, a song, monuments, and more.

The existence of countries implied the existence of something called "the national interest." People had varying opinions about this or that country and the nation-state system as a whole, but no one doubted the *existence* of this framework, or that a nation state was capable of pursuing its interests as a unit. People everywhere took this framework into account when they made relevant life decisions. If someone knew their travels were going to take them from one country to another, they'd know to bring along a passport as a matter of course.

Cyberspace

Technology and globalization are eroding that model. Nations still trade, but sovereign economic units now exist that are networks distributed across many countries and are as capable of agency as any social organism. Their decisions serve a self-interest only accidentally aligned with the "national interest" of any state. Self-interest implies the existence of a self. A country is such a self; but these newfangled selves are not countries. They're an emerging replacement for the idea of countries. Bitcoin is not the currency of any particular country. The Deep Web is a place policed by the authorities of no nation-state. To be sure, it doesn't exist in any physical place, it's in cyberspace but that's a place now, one that never existed before. Hackers physically situated in one so-called country can roam freely through the intercommunications of any other country, warping conversations and altering political processes as if national borders did not exist.

In this context, what was unthinkable a few decades ago is beginning to be thinkable. And not just thinkable but thought. For example, people calling themselves "sea-steaders" aspire to found communities without governments, floating in the oceans outside the jurisdiction of all nation-states, basing their survival on sovereignty as a product they can market, hoping to attract citizens through marketing, aspiring to be communities inhabited by customers, not citizens.

Just because it's thinkable doesn't mean it's do-able, of course, but thinkable is the fairy godmother of do-able. And sea-steaders are just one voice among many that are busy telling everybody what we should all be doing. This public conversation is always in progress, but today, there are so many voices talking at once, it sounds more like hubbub with each new voice joining in. The conversation is riotous because the topic matters. The erosion of any vital known system raises the question: what is the system? What are we all part of? No one has an answer to that question, but that's what the hubbub of voices is talking about. It's like a spirited conversation in a crowded room among people who speak different languages, a conversation in which no one waits their turn to speak.

Nature

Nation-states are only a few centuries old, at most. Much older are assumptions about the parts of the planet we humans do not inhabit. These were commonly known as "wilderness". Ever since Neolithic times, we have based our survival on altering the environment. Hunter-gatherers took what was there, and their way of life indeed depended on not altering the environment if they could help it, so that what they depended upon for survival would be there the next time they came through, just as it was before. But farmers cleared away brush and chopped down trees and dug up roots, so that they might replace what was there with crops they chose.

In this context, "taming the wilderness" must have registered axiomatically as a virtue. Anyone who "tamed wilderness" was doing a good thing, even a heroic thing. Until recent centuries, this assumption rarely came into question. There was so much wilderness that no one gave much thought to the possibility of humans using it all up. Even now, when the disappearance of wilderness is so palpably evidenced by objective statistics, taming the wilderness remains embedded in some cultures as a virtue. Until a scant few years ago (as of this writing) the government of Brazil took immense, declared satisfaction in cutting down the rainforest. That will have to change of course. When it does, things that seemed virtuous before will come to seem reprehensible. Culture will make sure of it. What those different values will be cannot be guessed from where we are now. But that's how culture changes what humans do, even in the face of contradictory demands from biology and genetics. It gets in there with values as its instrument and starts altering and shaping human decision-making.

Children

This, however, still only scrapes the surface of the change we're in. Until recently, every human community has presumed that producing children was a fundamental good. The more the better. Not perhaps for every individual but as a project for the whole group, absolutely yes: more children better, more children better—that was the persistent background hum. Evolution planted this mandate in us, because in evolutionary terms it made absolute sense: more progeny moves a species toward survival, fewer progeny moves it toward extinction. Culture produced values to support the drive we had to have, if we were to survive.

But this axiom—that maximizing our progeny is a good thing—no longer holds for humans. Now it's our soaring population that threatens our survival. And boy, is it ever threatening. Our sheer numbers might be making the planet uninhabitable by humans; and if that happens, we'll all be goners: no one will survive to remember that we ever existed at all. In this context, it's possible to question the morality of producing as many children as possible. Defending a woman's right to choose against pregnancy is (among other things) a way of saying, it's okay not to have more children. And that's only the beginning. What we do and what those actions mean depend on the narrative we're living in, and a culture's narrative is woven of values. Eventually, new values might have to form. A woman who decides not to have children might be regarded with reverence as someone who is siding with the planet and contributing to the survival of our species as a whole. Could such a value form and become ubiquitous? Maybe yes, maybe no: there's just no telling.

If it does happen, however, the transition won't be easy, because culture has been constructing values to support the biological mandate for millions of years. The anti-abortion movement is a direct backlash to the possibility of new values around this issue gaining ground. The idea that abortion must never take place is most commonly justified by labeling it murder, which moves abortion out of one narrative frame and into another. The question of avoiding species suicide doesn't come up in this other narrative frame. Here, the question becomes "Are we for murder or against it?" Framed this way, anti-abortion wins. No good person could be in favor of murder. But the thing is, people in the "pro-life" movement tend to oppose birth control as well. The unstated but implicit principle becomes discernable as: every human who can be born *should* be born.

Since this commandment is no doubt tethered to a deep biological urge, it has tremendous staying power. Culture, however, can veto or redirect biological urges as it deems necessary. This is probably the main reason why we've been successful as a species. We don't *have* to do whatever our genes tell us to. We can shape our own actions despite biology, using narratives and values as our wrenches and hammers. But can we master an urge as deep as this one, just with narratives and values? Can we build cultural values powerful enough to strike deals with an evolutionary urge to reproduce? Well, that's what is in play: that is a decision human culture is wrestling with today. I personally don't think genes can stop culture from figuring this one out. If culture weren't up to the challenge, family sizes would be about the same everywhere.

Machines

Technology takes a hand in this, because it secures us from most of the dangers that threatened the earliest humans. With technology, we can produce enough food for everyone. We can produce enough shelter, enough toys, enough everything. We can produce enough and too much of things we never dreamed of even wanting. Sharing the abundance is another matter, but producing it? That we've got down. The trouble is, we can only do it with energy extracted from finite resources, and (at this point) only in ways that pollute the environment and which might change the climate in ways catastrophic to the health of humans and other life forms. We don't know how else to do it. What's more, as matters stand, we don't know how to stop overproducing, because the only way to share the abundance among all of us is through jobs. If we stop overproducing, countless people will be out of work and end up in poverty and despair, and their opinions will be threads of the cultural fabric that emerges.

It's not just the consequences of this or that technology that challenges our narratives. It's technology itself putting pressure on the social paradigm we inherited from the past. For millions of years, technology was something we humans used to help us do our work. Two-plus centuries ago, give or take, technology became something that competed with humans, because they could do any physical work that needed to be done so much better than humans. After that, to a great extent, humans in the workplace became adjuncts to the machines: human work came to consist largely of inventing machines, building them, running them, fixing them, maintaining them.

Then came automation and fewer humans were needed to even run and service the machines. Then came robotics and artificial intelligence, which could replace humans doing many mental and even social jobs. Meanwhile, technology created so much of the physical and conceptual worlds we humans inhabit that it began to replace the human environment not just materially but conceptually. It generated whole worlds of intercommunication and exchange that we humans could no longer see because we were inside it: we couldn't observe it because we were made of it. It goes back to the aforementioned truism: the one thing the eye can't see is itself seeing.

The Digitized Life

Human selves, which form out of interaction with other humans, came to be mediated so largely by technology that relationships could exist entirely in virtual reality. The development of devices to replace human sense organs, although barely begun, is clearly moving forward. Digital devices driven by apps are shrinking so dramatically, they will soon be small enough to be injected into our bodies where they might serve various of our biological needs. All this raises serious questions about human identity. If devices are inside us and we are inside their world, remind me please: what exactly is a human again?

Technology raises the stakes on these issues because it now gives women the power to have babies or not have babies, whichever they wish. It detaches choice from biological mandate. Technology creates the birth control pill for women who don't want to get pregnant, it develops in vitro fertilization for those who do. Technology can begin a pregnancy in a lab, with no human parents involved except genetically: by joining an embryo provided by one donor to a sperm cell provided by another. Once a decision is possible, a decision must be made.

Gender

Technology goes deeper, however, than the biological underpinnings of human life. It's safe to say that, in every culture throughout history, one rock bottom assumption has been nearly universal. When it comes to identity, gender is the first fact. That, you're born into. Whatever decisions you make after birth, you have to start with that first fact: you're either born male or you're born female.

But that is no longer the first fact, because technology has entered the picture. Technology enables a person born into a body associated with one gender to switch to a body associated with the other. Technology makes gender a choice—only to a limited extent, at this point, to be sure; but you know how it is with that old devil, technology. Once it gets started on a project, it doesn't quit till it's done. If we survive long enough, it seems perfectly plausible that it will make gender vanish as a category of human life.

Culture

In this matter, however, technology has to contend with culture. Every culture on the planet has a deeply rooted story about the difference between male and female. Men are like this, women are like that. So says every culture, or at least every culture so far. Based on its gender-story, culture assigns roles to the characters. The females will be up for the girl parts, the males for the boy parts. The story will be about the complications that beset them as they struggle to play their assigned parts. It might be comic, it might be tragic, but it'll be enough like stories one knows, that one will be able to ad lib one's part. When the story changes, however, new questions come up. Like: "What is my assigned part now? Am I playing the hero or the villain? How does any of this fit into the story? Incidentally, what *is* the story?"

In this context, phrases that went unnoticed a few years ago now attract comment because people don't automatically agree on what they mean. "Be a man," used to mean something like rise-to-a-noble-stature. Now it identifies the speaker as something of a brute. "Woman's work" used to signify disrespect for a category of work; now its use expresses a disrespect for women in general. The year I graduated from college, a romantic movie swept America, an instant classic called *The Graduate*. In the end, the woman in this movie is trying to marry someone and the man bursts in and messes up the wedding and drags her away and gets her onto a bus and it's great: they're together. The End. I read a review of that movie recently that saw the main character as something of a stalker. The meaning of the movie has changed because the context has changed. And let's not even get started on the Rock Hudson-Doris Day movies of the previous decade, which dramatized the essence of romance as the man not-taking-no-for-an-answer.

But in a world where people are looking for romantic relationships, they need some shared understanding of what "romantic" means. And when all the meanings are changing, how do they form this shared understanding?

Togetherness

What's more, the search for relationships is changing its significance. This search used to be the process of finding the partner one would marry so that one could start a family. "Family", however, no longer has one fixed meaning. Of course, it was always true that family had different meanings in different cultures. Within each culture, however, there was some common general understanding of the word; the culture's single-wholeness demanded as much. In some cultures, back in those long-ago times, a few decades ago, "family" meant a heterosexual couple and their several children living together without other relatives. In other cultures, "family" meant one man and his (possibly several) wives plus their brood of children along with some odds and ends of relatives, all living together. There were many forms of family around the world, but whatever form it took in any culture, family tended to include blood-kinship as part of its meaning. And in every culture, it tended to include some connotation of warmth and safety.

In my lifetime this began to change. When I was a young adult, communes emerged, full of unrelated people who called themselves families. It was considered radical at the time. Today, in America. there are single-mother households, single-father households, blended families, cluster-of-partners families who have no children, same-sex parent families with adopted children, families of more than one couple, heterosexual couples living with their children... The forms of family were always numerous around the planet, but now, numerous different forms of family might exist within the same culture—within American culture, for example.

With the meaning of family up in the air, the purpose of dating detaches from its original meaning. If it's not about finding the person you're going to marry, what is it about? Without kinship, is the warmth-and-safety part achievable? How so? It must be hard to build a family if it's not clear what "a family" is. A survey I read recently showed millennials to be the loneliest generation. I wasn't surprised. Then I read that millennials were no longer thought to be the loneliest generation: that title now went Gen-Z. I bet they've given ground, however, to a newer loneliest generation, whatever one's just coming into adulthood now.

The Story We Are In

I know I haven't listed everything that's changing, not just in the unfolding story but in the stage upon which the world-story is unfolding. Others might draw up the list differently. They almost surely would, in fact, But I'm pretty sure most people feel there's a list to draw up. That's a place to start, because that at least is a feeling we have in common. But we have to realize: because of the way that narrative works and because of the times in which we live, we're not seeing one another's lists, and we *have* to see one another's lists. It's no use arguing about them until we can see them.

So how do we combat Truther Narrative? Good question. Someone wrote to me recently to tell me that her husband's granddaughter had become a believer in the Q-Anon Truther Narrative. She asked if I could point her to some magazines, some websites, some evidence, some information, some anything that would prove to this young woman that the story was false. I had nothing to tell her. Truther Narrative is impervious to evidence. It is non-falsifiable. It is a narrative that feeds certain hungers. The only way to combat Truther Narratives is to abate those hungers better than Truther Narrative can do.

Truther Narrative *is* a narrative—that's the first and most important point. The only way to combat a narrative is with a more powerful narrative. If we're not victims of a secret powerful cabal, who are we? If the evil force we're rallying to defeat doesn't exist, what should we be doing about the harm that is actually out there and coming at us? The narrative that defeats Truther Narrative has to tell a story that speaks to people's actual experiences. It has to acknowledge some similar experience we're all going through in our multitude of different ways. The narrative has to tap the power of metaphor, tap the music already playing inside us. It must draw in everyone, or what's the point? Because what that narrative needs to do, in the end, is to awaken into consciousness the one-whole-self that we humans are.

What does this require? It requires, first of all, that we discern the story we are actually in. Truther Narrative can get away with making stuff up; we can't. We have to build this story by telling it to one another as we're in the very process of discerning it. Let's get everyone in on the quest. What's really going on? Everyone should be part of this conversation. No one knows everything, but everyone knows something.

What's the opposite of Truther Narrative? First of all, it's accepting that we live in history. Yeah: that messy thing. The river we're in is the river we're in. Pointless to wish we were in some other river, we have to deal with this one, which means, study the currents, learn to paddle and steer, figure out how to negotiate with the complexity of it all. Yes, unfortunately, the complexity of it all.

And we can only do this piecemeal. That's hard to accept but it's true. No one can do everything, each person can do something. Everyone wishes they could wake up tomorrow in a perfect world, but none of us will. Building a better world than the one we're in will take all of us believing that if we each do what we can, it will somehow all add up. I have a fond hope that the world-wide tumult and confusion of the present day is simply what it looks like from the inside when the creature we might call humanity-as-a-whole is waking up to an awareness of itself as a whole. Truther Narrative works against this project fundamentally, by trying to coagulate humans into ever smaller, non-overlapping groups. It tries to keep the whole of humanity from waking up to its own singleness. That's why all of us who reject Truther Narrative must get busy constructing that counternarrative. Superman doesn't exist so it's up to us mortals to get the job done.

Politics can facilitate this work or it can impede this work, but politics alone can't get this job done. Politicians can build structures but only with the bricks that culture provides. Culture is what gives groups of humans the sense of peoplehood they need to carry out social projects together: culture is what enables disparate people to form group intentions, and craft plans together, and exercise agency.

The trouble is, throughout human history, our species has existed as many cultures, each with its own social coherence, its own quality of single-whole-ness. Until recently, when people of different cultures have interacted, they've had to go through a process of some sort in order to become intercommunicative. At a crude level, this has involved at least learning one another's language—which takes time.

Sometimes constant intermingling has led to the emergence of a new polyglot language understood by both groups—but that takes time. Sometimes two cultures abutting on one another have interacted in the frontier zone where they overlap, enough so to develop a sense of one another's whole context, thereby unlocking a higher level of mutual understanding—but that takes time. Just look how long a sentence it takes to even get the whole thought said.

Sometimes pervasive interaction over a long period of time has resulted in two very different cultures becoming two (still-very-different) parts of the same larger culture. This is great when it happens, and it's what must happen in the largest sense. We don't need a global culture we share *instead of* all our different cultures…We need a global culture we share in *addition* to all our different cultures. Such a meta-culture can never form overnight, however, because it can never come into being by fiat. A global culture we share can develop only out of countless individual interactions and conversations—which takes time.

Yes, rare towering individuals can have huge historical effects. And yes, individuals possessed of tremendous social power—billionaires, generals, autocrats, charismatic "party leaders", criminal overlords, monarchs, and the like—can issue commands and use force to make big changes happen by fiat very suddenly. But these are structural changes, institutional changes. The cultural cooking-together that follows (if it does), happens over a longer period of time, as a result of many, small, unrecorded individual transactions known only to the few people directly involved.

This then is our dilemma. We're plowing through the 21st century needing a single world-scale human culture, a context in which any of us can meet and talk and understand any of us; but as a species, we're still organized as many different cultures that are aesthetically and emotionally unintelligible to one another. And many evolutionary psychologists believe we're biologically incapable of having a shared culture of our own without having another culture to recognize as Other. How can we short-circuit this tendency of ours, if we have it, and especially if it's genetically embedded?

The Noise

In the past, different cultures were largely separated from one another by geography. One culture lived over here, another over there, and between them was a border where they interacted and sometime overlapped a little. If a blending-process occurred at all, it happened in these zones of overlap.

Now, however, information and communication technology has generated landscapes that never existed before, such as cyberspace. Here, everybody connected to the global network of human interactivity might encounter anybody connected to the global network: let me say it again for emphasis: anybody and everybody might encounter anybody and everybody. This has never before been the case.

Consequently, all over the world, but especially in the most technologically developed societies, people are now exposed, constantly, persistently, and simultaneously to a multitude of different cultures in their everyday life. If you're in a building with a hundred rooms, in each of which a band is playing a different song, you can go from room to room and hear music in each one. But if you're in a single big room in which all those bands are playing at once, you're apt to hear noise, not music. The global culture we so urgently need has to form in this single big room bursting with noise.

And how can it? As humans we seem to have an intolerance for noise and an appetite for music. More noise intensifies our craving for music. Cultural incoherence fuels a desire for cultural coherence. The culture-noise enabled and intensified by technology fuels identity politics, culture wars, fragmentation, and social bubbles. because our basic human needs include a desire to be among people among whom one feels at home.

The Music

None of us as individuals can create a new culture because that's not how culture works. Culture creates itself through people's ongoing, daily interactions with one another. If you know what to look for, I think you can spot many indications that a world culture is trying to be born. It will take a paradigm shift on a global scale, so it's hard to see anything but chaos in the unsyncopated conversations of our current era. But if we're aware that a paradigm shift is happening, and if we have some understanding of *how* it's happening, perhaps we can, each in our own small way, contribute something useful to its birth.

Recently, I saw a video installation at the San Francisco Museum of Modern Art called *The Visitors*, created by Icelandic performance artist Ragnar Kjartansson. Kjartansson invited eight friends to a big ramshackle house out in the countryside, somewhere in New England. There, he filmed himself and his friends playing music in separate rooms. The hour-long film was projected on nine screens in a single long, dark chamber. When I arrived, the nine films were all running, each one a film of a musician alone in a room, playing music, one on a piano, one on an accordion, one on a cello, one on a set of drums… The artist himself was in the bathroom, taking a bath, and playing an acoustic guitar. The room with the nine screens was huge and warm and humid, and the ceiling was so high it was lost into the darkness. I was one of fifty or sixty people taking in this experience. If you went close to one of the nine screens you'd hear that music more, and if you went close to another you'd hear that music mainly, the sound from the other screens receding into the background.

The room was crowded but the only light was from the nine movies. The people around me were shadows. Some of them were murmuring to each other, but the only sound I could hear was the music from the movies. At first I thought the nine musicians were each playing their own music, but I noticed that they were all wearing headphones, whereupon I realized: they could hear each other. They were playing together, alone in their separate rooms. Their music began rising to a crescendo. They started singing, and as the lyrics emerged, the metaphor swamped me. For a moment there, I saw it. This was it. We could do this. All of humanity on Earth—alone in the eight billion rooms of our separate lives, alone in the separate mansions of our countless social bubbles, alone in the togetherness of our various different cultures—we could do this. We don't know how yet, but we're learning. All of us will one day be making music together, not just noise. We have to figure out how, and it takes time, but we're learning. We can do this.

References and Further Reading

Aaronovitch, David: *Voodoo Histories, The Role of the Conspiracy Theory in Shaping Modern History.* Penguin Random House, 2009.

Brotherton, Rob: *Suspicious Minds, Why We Believe Conspiracy Theories.* Bloomsbury Sigma, New York, 2017.

Burman, Edward: *The Templars, Knights of God.* Destiny Books, Rochester, Vermont, 1986.

Clark McCauley and Susan Jacques: *The Popularity of Conspiracy Theories of Presidential. Assassination: A Bayesian Analysis.* Journal of Personality, Volume 37 May 1979.

Conan, Eric: *The Secrets of an Antisemitic Manipulation.* L'Express November 24, 1999 (available online at http://www.lexpress.presse.fr/editorial/zooms/protocole/ouverture.htm

Cubitt, Geoffrey: *The Jesuit Myth: Conspiracy Theory and Politics in Nineteenth Century France.* Clarendon Press, Oxford, 1993.

Fenster, Mark: *Conspiracy Theories: Secrecy and Power in American Culture.* University of Minnesota Press, Minneapolis, 2008.

Foster, Joshua D. and Shrira, Ilan: *Personality Paranoia, 9/11, and the roots of conspiracy theories,* Psychology Today. September 11, 2008.

Goertzel, Ted. *Belief in Conspiracy Theories.* Political Psychology 15: 733-744, 1994.

Graumann, C. F. and Moscovici S. (editors) *Changing Conceptions of Conspiracy,* Springer Series in Social Psychology: Springer Verlag, 1987.

Hofstadter, Richard: *The Paranoid Style in American Politics.* Vintage (reprint), New York, 2008.

Howarth, Stephen. *The Knights Templar.* Atheneum, 1982.

Knight , Peter: *Conspiracy Nation: The Politics of Paranoia in Postwar America.* New York University Press, New Yori, 2002.

McGowan, Kathleen: *Conspiracy Theories Explained.* Psychology Today, November 01, 2004.

McIntosh, C., *The Rose Cross and the Age of Reason: 18th-century Rosicrucianism in Central Europe and Its Relationship to the Enlightenment,* E.J. Brill: Leiden, 1997.

McIntosh, C., *The Rose Cross and the Age of Reason: 18th-century Rosicrucianism in Central Europe and Its Relationship to the Enlightenment.* E.J.Brill: Leiden, 1997.

McIntosh, C., *The Rosicrucians,* Crucible/Thorsons, Wellingborough, 1980.

Merland, Anna: *Republic of Lies: American Conspiracy Theorists and Their Surprising Rise to Power.* Metropolitan Book, New York, 2019.

Pipes, Daniel: *Conspiracy: How the Paranoid Style Flourishes and Where It Comes From.* Touchstone (Simon & Schuster), New York, 1999.

Ralls, K., *The Templars & the Grail: Knights of the Quest,* Quest Books, Chicago, 2003.

Roberts, John M. *The Mythology of the Secret Societies,* Watkins, London. 2008.

Rosenblum Nancy L. (and Muirhead, Russell: *A Lot of People Are Saying: The New Conspiracism and the Assault on Democracy.* Princeton University Press, 2019.

Skinner, Patricia (editor): *Jews in Medieval Britain: Historical, Literary and Archaeological Perspectives Hardcover*. Boydell Press, Suffolk, England, 2003.

Smith, Helmut Walser: *The Butcher's Tale: Murder and Anti-semitism in a German town* Norton, New York, 2002.

Yates, F.A., *Rosicrucian Enlightenment*. Routledge and Kegan Paul: London, 1972.

On the web:

Nesta H. Webster's *Secret Societies* is described and discussed at *http://freemasonry.bcy.ca/anti-masonry/anti-masonry06.html#protocols*

A history of *The protocols of the Elders of Zion* can be found at http://freemasonry.bcy.ca/anti-masonry/anti-masonry06.html#protocols

John Robison's *Proofs of a Conspiracy*—the complete text—is available at http://www.sacred-texts.com/

"Origins of Freemasonry"—a lecture delivered in Scotland by Robert Lomas University of Bradford in 2000 is of some interest as an example of a modern attempt to link templars to freemasons. -- http://www.robertlomas.com/Freemason/Origins.html

Adam Weishaupt and the Illuminati are discussed at https://freemasonry.bcy.ca/texts/illuminati.html

About blood libel through history: https://encyclopedia.ushmm.org/content/en/article/blood-libel

Tamim Ansary was born in Kabul, Afghanistan, to an American mother and an Afghan father. His life has straddled the fault line between the Western and Islamic Worlds, giving him an enduring interest in the relation between cultural reality and objective reality. His early career in the textbook industry gave him a particular interest in world history and the role of narrative in that biggest of all stories. As a freelance writer, he contributed chapters to half a dozen of the major world history programs used in American high schools at that time. In the aftermath of 9/11 he wrote *Destiny Disrupted: A History of the World Through Islamic Eyes*, and later *The Invention of Yesterday*, which looks at world history as a fabric woven of narratives. In 2006, Susan Hoffman, director of the Osher Lifelong Learning Institute (OLLI) at San Francisco State University invited him to present a series of lectures on conspiracy theory. In 2012, he was invited to offer the course again, at U.C. Berkeley's OLLI program and then again in 2020. The author wishes to express his gratitude to Ms. Hoffman and to the OLLI community of lifelong learners for their support and interest.

Made in the USA
Las Vegas, NV
14 November 2024

11179733R00098